T0340212

PENGUIN  CLASSICS

# SELECTED POEMS

Victor Hugo (1802–1885) was the most forceful, prolific, and versatile of French nineteeth-century writers. He wrote Romantic costume dramas, many volumes of lyrical and satirical verse, political and other journalism, criticism, and several novels, the best known of which are *Les Misérables* (1862) and the youthful *Notre Dame de Paris* (1831). A royalist and conservative as a young man, Hugo later became a committed social democrat and during the Second Empire of Napoleon III was exiled from France, living in the Channel Islands. He returned to Paris in 1870 and remained a great public figure until his death: his body lay in state under the Arc de Triomphe before being buried in the Panthéon.

Brooks Haxton is the author of five selections of poetry. Among his translations are *Dances for Flute and Thunder: Poems from the Ancient Greek,* which was nominated for the PEN translation award, and *Fragments: The Collected Wisdom of Heraclitus.* He lives in Syracuse, New York.

# VICTOR HUGO
## SELECTED POEMS

*Translated and with an Introduction*
*by Brooks Haxton*

PENGUIN BOOKS

PENGUIN BOOKS

Published by the Penguin Group

Penguin Group (USA) Inc., 375 Hudson Street, New York, New York 10014, U.S.A.

Penguin Group (Canada), 90 Eglinton Avenue East, Suite 700, Toronto,
Ontario, Canada M4P 2Y3 (a division of Pearson Penguin Canada Inc.)

Penguin Books Ltd, 80 Strand, London WC2R 0RL, England

Penguin Ireland, 25 St Stephen's Green, Dublin 2, Ireland (a division of Penguin Books Ltd)

Penguin Group (Australia), 250 Camberwell Road, Camberwell,
Victoria 3124, Australia (a division of Pearson Australia Group Pty Ltd)

Penguin Books India Pvt Ltd, 11 Community Centre, Panchsheel Park, New Delhi – 110 017, India

Penguin Group (NZ), cnr Airborne and Rosedale Roads,
Albany, Auckland 1310, New Zealand (a division of Pearson New Zealand Ltd)

Penguin Books (South Africa) (Pty) Ltd, 24 Sturdee Avenue,
Rosebank, Johannesburg 2196, South Africa

Penguin Books Ltd, Registered Offices: 80 Strand, London WC2R 0RL, England

First published in Penguin Books 2002

Translation, introduction, and selection copyright © Brooks Haxton, 2002
All rights reserved

The translator would like to thank the editors of the following publications where
parts of this book have appeared: *American Poetry Review*, the Introduction,
"Oceano Nox," "My Two Girls," "All Souls' Day, 1846," "When We Were
Living," "Little Song," "The Graveyard at Villequier," "Word from the Dunes,"
"During Sickness," "The Trumpet of Judgment," from "The Art of Being a
Grandfather, Lesson One: The Moon," and "Sonnet"; *American Scholar*, "Boaz
Asleep"; *Hudson Review*, "As I Have Set My Lip," "Nights in June," "Napoleon's
Army After the Fall of Moscow," "Barefoot," "Letter from Normandy," and
"How It Happened"; *Paris Review*, "Mugitusque Boum," "Et Nox Facta Est,"
and "The Plume of Satan."

LIBRARY OF CONGRESS CATALOGING IN PUBLICATION DATA
Hugo, Victor, 1802–1885.
[Poems. English & French. Selections]
Selected poems / Victor Hugo; translated and with an introduction
by Brooks Haxton.
p. cm.
ISBN 0-14-243703-4 (pbk.)
I. Haxton, Brooks, 1950–   II. Title.
PQ2283 .A48 2002
841'.7—dc21    2001044802

Set in Stempel Garamond

146056540

*Ceci est le sac du semeur.*
*Prenez et jetez au vent.*

This is the grainsack.
Take and scatter on the wind.

# CONTENTS

# INTRODUCTION

EXACTLY TWO HUNDRED YEARS AGO, while Napoleon flourished at the first height of his dictatorial power, Victor-Marie Hugo was born with weak limbs and a large head. His mother had little interest in her three boys, least of all in him, whose sickliness she found repugnant. Bored with her husband, a carpenter's son risen through the ranks of the Republican army, she abandoned her family and went to live in Paris with her husband's superior officer. Later, she came back and left again, came back, and left, finally, with the children.

The baby, which one doctor said would need a miracle to survive, died eighty-three years later, an old man well known for his stamina and for the vigor of his mind and body. For most of his life he was the most famous writer in the world. His legacy includes the century's most celebrated works of drama, fiction, memoir, criticism, and poetry. Because his novels *Les Misérables* and *The Hunchback of Notre Dame* have now entered their third century of continuous success, we may forget that Hugo was a poet first. His poems have been judged by many great writers among the finest in French, though for several generations they have been neglected in France and virtually unknown to readers of English.

Of course, no serious reader would consider such a lapse at all reliable as a measure of the poems themselves. The best of Shakespeare's sonnets, for example, seem to us among the finest poems ever written, but we know that almost no one for two hundred years appreciated them. Even a poet as keen on sonnets as William Wordsworth wrote that the twenty-eight poems at the end of Shakespeare's sequence are "worthless" because of their "sameness, tediousness, quaintness, and obscurity." This supposedly worthless group includes many masterpieces. Wordsworth's inability to read those poems resembles our own recent obliviousness to the poetry of Hugo.

Hugo himself, as one of the most influential critics of Shakespeare, argued that shifts in the history of tastes and styles accounted for audiences' difficulty with *Lear*. The play in its original form had been restored to the stage in Hugo's lifetime after a two-hundred-year hiatus. We no longer need the world's most famous writer to lead us past our prejudices into an awareness of Shakespeare's greatest writing. But we may need a critic of Hugo's stature to help us see Hugo. The passionate vision in the poems themselves will take us past a superficial sense of datedness, but only if we feel the greater receptivity and practice the sharper attention that good writing celebrates.

During his exile on Guernsey, as a leader in the opposition to Napoleon III, Hugo often wrote a hundred lines of poetry per day. From the cot in his study, which was a solarium overlooking the sea, Hugo rose every day before dawn, drank cold coffee from the night before, and stood at his table writing until noon. After a five-course lunch, with several fine wines from his private cellar, he spent two hours hiking, in sunshine or full gale, and swimming in the sea. In the afternoon he returned to work long into the evening. Then, late at night, he ate an even larger meal with his mistress, for whom he had bought the neighboring house, and went to sleep.

*Œuvres Poétiques Complètes,* without the plays in verse or the far vaster prose, is half again the length of the complete Shakespeare, enough to fill ten volumes as thick as *The Complete Poems of Emily Dickinson*. At Guernsey alone, Hugo wrote twice as many lines as Whitman wrote in his whole life. Meanwhile, he also wrote the vast *Les Misérables* and thousands more pages of prose.

Though much of Hugo is overwritten, the best of it still represents in French "a kind of superhuman power," in the words of Jean Paul Sartre, who judges Hugo as a poet "unquestionably the sovereign of the whole century." Hugo's loosening of the strictures of French poetry is distinct even to a foreign ear. He used common words, without the so-called nobility of poets before him. He broke new ground in his direct engagement with personal experience; for example, in the straightforwardness of the exposition in the opening of this poem about the massacre of 1851:

The boy had taken two shots in the head . . .
Speechless, his gray lips fell open. Death
had drowned out in his eye the last wild look.
His arms hung limp, as if they needed to be held.
He had in his pocket a boxwood top and string.
My forefinger would have fit in either wound.
Have you seen blackberries bleed? His skull
had been punched through easily as punkwood.

By the time he wrote this poem in his forties, Hugo was the most famous writer in France, the host of the most renowned salon, a personal friend of the former king, a member of the Academy, and a peer. Still, he considered himself a poet of the people. Six months before the coup of 1851, he denounced his former friend, Louis Bonaparte, as an enemy of freedom. On December 3, at the beginning of the violence in which more than four hundred men, women, and children were shot dead by Bonaparte's soldiers, the famous poet climbed the steps of the Bastille and made a passionate plea to the army to join the people in their resistance to tyranny. His mistress begged him to come down before he was shot, and he shouted back, "I am willing to die for the cause of freedom."

The self-glorification in this moment of bona fide heroism is distinct. Hugo's eagerness to celebrate his own accomplishments and virtues is legendary. He declared repeatedly in old age that his poems would live as long as the French language itself, a claim some may find the more distasteful because it is true.

His work expanded in all directions the range of subject matters and tones admitted into French poetry. He wrote with passion about history, erotic experience, familial love, philosophy, nature, social justice, art, and mysticism. This range of interests, his enormous vocabulary, and his singular skill in various styles make him the most protean of all French poets.

Without having read the celebrations of childhood in the poems of Blake and Wordsworth, Hugo discovered children as a subject for poetry in France. Some of his best poems were written in memory of his daughter Leopoldine, who, six months after she was married at the age of nineteen, drowned with her husband in a boating accident, believed by some to be a suicide:

> Consider how, in doubt, my Lord, in suffering,
> with eyes too full of tears, gone blind, plunged
> into the blackest depth of grief, in sight of nothing,
> wracked, a mind might lose its blessedness . . .
>
> My God, I understand it, that the man is mad
>     who dares object.
> I quit accusing you. I quit the cursing.
>     Please, though, let me cry!
>
> At least let tears still blur my sight,
> since you designed the flesh for this!
> Just let me lean against this stone and ask
> my child if she can feel that I am here.

These translations mean, above all, to communicate intensity of feeling. French poetry after Villon and Ronsard turned from dramatic energy toward wit and ideal beauty, with rigorous attention to sound, diction, and lucidity of style. Hugo was master of these strict conventions, winning a prize from the French Academy at the age of fifteen. Even so, intense dramatic energy characterized his poems almost from the start, as André Gide has written about the second book, *Les Orientales,* published when the poet was twenty-seven: "Everything is there—strength, grace, a smile, and the most moving sobs . . . What a poetic earthquake!"

Hugo's sensory and dramatic acuity take his poems beyond traditional beauty into a sublime inclusiveness and energy still thrilling to the modern reader. This later poem, for example, dwells on the erotic charge in the biblical story of Ruth's visit to Boaz sleeping:

> Ruth was dreaming. Boaz slept. The grass looked black.
> And little bells of sheep were trembling on the verge

of silence. Goodness came down clear as starlight
into the great calm where the lions go to drink.

All slept, all, from Ur to Bethlehem.
The stars enameled the deep black of the sky.
A narrow crescent in the low dark
of the West shone, while Ruth wondered,

lying still now, eyes half opened,
under the twinging of their lids, what god
of the eternal summer passing dropped
his golden scythe there in that field of stars.

Hugo's friend Sainte-Beuve, a minor poet and one of the century's most powerful literary critics, was an early champion of Hugo's work. But when Sainte-Beuve and Madame Hugo entered into a longtime sexual liaison in September 1831, the critic began to cast aspersions on Hugo's writings and character.

Until this betrayal, Hugo seems to have been monogamous. His first mistress, the actress Juliette Drouet, remained his companion for fifty years until she died in his arms. While maintaining his arrangements with his wife and mistress, he also had many hundreds of brief sexual encounters. One young woman whom he saw for several months was Sarah Bernhardt, shortly thereafter to become the world's most celebrated actress. She was twenty-six and he, in his seventies, was maintaining a simultaneous affair with the beautiful, already married daughter of his old friend, the poet Théophile Gautier. Judith Gautier was later an inspiration to Wagner and a prominent woman of letters in her own right. Hugo speaks in the following sonnet to Judith Gautier and publishes the poem as a direct challenge to conventional assumptions:

Death and Beauty, being deep, the both of them,
both jeweled with obsidian and azure, I would say
the two were sisters, fierce and rich
with the same promise, and enigma. Women,

shine to me!—voices, glances, black hair,
blond—for I am dying! I, who see your brilliance,
like the sheen of pearls that tumble in the breakers,
or like birds that flash far off in a dark woods.

Judith, our two fates have brought us closer
than we seem, to see your face and mine;
in your eyes a divine abyss appears, and I feel

in my soul a gulf plunged through with stars;
both of us belong to that same sky,
since you are beautiful and I am old.

When Hugo died, he lay in state under the Arc de Triomphe, the whole of which was draped for the occasion in black velvet. He was mourned by millions, a crowd larger, it was said, than the entire population of Paris. Then attacks on his work and on his character became more and more common, first in France and later in other countries. After his death, Hugo, already a controversial figure, was much more widely attacked and much more seldom defended.

But however real the weaknesses in Hugo's character, including his obvious self-indulgence and vanity, and however stirring his heroism at the ramparts in 1851 and again after his return to Paris during the troubles of 1871, finally, we judge him as a writer by the work. His poetry, to many of the best writers in France, appears unsurpassed. As for its moral character, his writing did as much as anyone's to expose the horrors of capital punishment, poverty, and social injustice.

For the past century, Hugo as a poet has been absent from the minds of American readers. These translations are an effort to bring speakers of English closer to an amazing poet and human presence. Without his groundbreaking genius, others like Baudelaire, Rimbaud, and those who followed in France and elsewhere could not have written as they did. Much of what seems best in twentieth-century American poetry would have been inconceivable, and the world of imagination would have been less rich and free.

As Baudelaire wrote in 1861, even before the publication of much of Hugo's most exploratory later work:

When you think of what French poetry was before he appeared and what a rejuvenation it has undergone since his arrival, when you imagine how insignificant it would have been if he had not appeared, how many deep and mysterious feelings which have been put into words would have remained unexpressed, how many intelligent minds he has brought into being . . . it is impossible not to consider him as one of those rare and providential minds who in the domain of literature bring about the salvation of us all. . . .

# A NOTE ON THE TRANSLATION

I HAVE BEGUN by trying to find in English the most effective literal rendition of the French. Most of my versions stay close to the phrasing of the originals.

The main difference between Hugo's verse and my versions may be my enjambment of lines that Hugo stopped with terminal punctuation. Because the end-stopped line has not been required in English as strictly as in French, to observe French practice of another era ignores the disposition of an ear for poetry in English. What my overflowing line has lost in fidelity to outward form it gains by its fidelity to the suppleness and muscularity of Hugo's style.

Similarly, for American readers more accustomed to free verse, strict meter and rhyme may misrepresent the tone of a writer whose fluency loosened the alexandrine. Free verse, on the other hand, misses the tenor of Hugo's formal mastery. My rule of thumb has been to write iambically with no equivalent measure. In place of rhyme, deliberate assonance and consonance sustain the verbal music.

Since the dramatic vitality of verbal music is almost never reproduced in paraphrase, I have pared down especially where the effectiveness of a lofty tone depends on Hugo's genius for French verse. Often my omissions involve rhetorical figures that feel strained in literal English. Notes say where these changes have been most conspicuous.

While avoiding quaintness, I have tried to find in English the flavor of Hugo's French. Where liberties serve my version of the poem, I have altered and substituted freely. I have also omitted words or phrases, in some cases sentences at a stretch, that in English fail to suggest the intensity of the original poem.

The greatest possible success for my versions, at their strictest and their freest, is to suggest the power of Hugo's imagination and, I hope, to send my readers back to him in his own language.

# VICTOR HUGO
## SELECTED POEMS

*Le toit s'égaye et rit.*
André Chénier.

Lorsque l'enfant paraît, le cercle de famille
Applaudit à grands cris. Son doux regard qui brille
  Fait briller tous les yeux,
Et les plu tristes fronts, les plus souillés peut-être,
Se dérident soudain à voir l'enfant paraître,
  Innocent et joyeux.

Soit que juin ait verdi mon seuil, ou que novembre
Fasse autour d'un grand feu vacillant dans la chambre
  Les chaises se toucher,
Quand l'enfant vient, la joie arrive et nous éclaire.
On rit, on se récrie, on l'appelle, et sa mère
  Tremble à le voir marcher.

Quelquefois nous parlons, en remuant la flamme,
De patrie et de Dieu, des poètes, de l'âme
  Qui s'élève en priant;
L'enfant paraît, adieu le ciel et la patrie
Et les poètes saints! la grave causerie
  S'arrête en souriant.

La nuit, quand l'homme dort, quand l'esprit rêve, à l'heure
Où l'on entend gémir, comme une voix qui pleure,
  L'onde entre les roseaux,
Si l'aube tout à coup là-bas luit comme un phare,
Sa clarté dans les champs éveille une fanfare
  De cloches et d'oiseaux.

Enfant, vous êtes l'aube et mon âme est la plaine
Qui des plus douces fleurs embaume son haleine
  Quand vous la respirez;

*One-Year-Old*

When he arrived, the family clapped their hands
and called to him. His sweet look
   made our looks more tender.
Even the saddest, the most haggard
face would smile to see him
   innocent and happy.

With June green at the threshhold, or November
splashing firelight on the hearth, chairs
   drawn close by evening,
when he came, his joy contained us in its clarity:
we laughed, we called to him, his mother caught
   her breath to see him walk.

Sometimes, stirring up the fire, we spoke
about great causes: justice, truth, and art,
   souls stirred by passion;
but, when he arrived, our high talk stopped—
God, Art, and the Republic—all
   suspended in a smile.

As if, at night, when every mind must sleep,
in dreams where waves among the reeds make
   low sobs like a woman's voice,
as if dawn swept up like a beacon
over the wide fields, rousing into fanfare
   all the great bells and the songbirds—

child! you are that dawn to me, and in my soul
wildflowers steeped in sunlight breathe their balm
   when your breath brushes mine.

Mon âme est la forêt dont les sombres ramures
S'emplissent pour vous seul de suaves murmures
   Et de rayons dorés!

Car vos beaux yeux sont pleins de douceurs infinies,
Car vos petites mains, joyeuses et bénies,
   N'ont point mal fait encor;
Jamais vos jeunes pas n'ont touché notre fange,
Tête sacrée! enfant aux cheveux blonds! bel ange
   A l'auréole d'or!

Vous êtes parmi nous la colombe de l'arche.
Vos pieds tendres et purs n'ont point l'âge où l'on marche,
   Vos ailes sont d'azur.
Sans le comprendre encor vous regardez le monde.
Double virginité! corps où rien n'est immonde,
   Ame où rien n'est impur!

Il est si beau, l'enfant, avec son doux sourire,
Sa douce bonne foi, sa voix qui veut tout dire,
   Ses pleurs vite apaisés,
Laissant errer sa vue étonnée et ravie,
Offrant de toutes parts sa jeune âme à la vie
   · Et sa bouche aux baisers!

Seigneur! préservez-moi, préservez ceux que j'aime,
Frères, parents, amis, et mes ennemis même
    Dans le mal triomphants,
De jamais voir, Seigneur! l'été sans fleurs vermeilles,
La cage sans oiseaux, la ruche sans abeilles,
   La maison sans enfants!

*18 mai 1830.*

In these dark woods in me black branches
burgeon for you only, and turn gold at sunrise,
    filling with sweet murmurs.

Because your eyes are infinitely tender,
because your small hands, joyful, wholly blessed,
    have wronged no one ever,
your steps never touch our filth, your head
is sacred, your blond hair makes visible
    the aura of angelic thought.

You see a world beyond mere understanding.
In your body nothing is unclean, nothing
    in your soul impure!
Your gaze, astonished, ravished, wanders—
everywhere you offer up your soul to life
    and your mouth to kisses!

Lord, keep me, and keep the ones I love,
my brothers, kinsmen, friends—worst enemies:
    preserve us from the hell
of summer unsurprised by flowers, from the bare cage
without songbirds, from the hive the bees deserted,
    and the house unvisited by children.

Puisque j'ai mis ma lèvre à ta coupe encor pleine,
Puisque j'ai dans tes mains posé mon front pâli,
Puisque j'ai respiré parfois la douce haleine
De ton âme, parfum dans l'ombre enseveli,

Puisqu'il me fut donné de t'entendre me dire
Les mots où se répand le cœur mystérieux,
Puisque j'ai vu pleurer, puisque j'ai vu sourire
Ta bouche sur ma bouche et tes yeux sur mes yeux;

Puisque j'ai vu briller sur ma tête ravie
Un rayon de ton astre, hélas! voilé toujours,
Puisque j'ai vu tomber dans l'onde de ma vie
Une feuille de rose arrachée à tes jours,

Je puis maintenant dire aux rapides années:
—Passez! passez toujours! je n'ai plus à vieillir!
Allez-vous-en avec vos fleurs toutes fanées;
J'ai dans l'âme une fleur que nul ne peut cueillir!

Votre aile en le heurtant ne fera rien répandre
Du vase où je m'abreuve et que j'ai bien rempli.
Mon âme a plus de feu que vous n'avez de cendre!
Mon cœur a plus d'amour que vous n'avez d'oubli!

*1er janvier 1835. Minuit et demi.*

*As I Have Set My Lip*

As I have set my lip to your still brimming cup,
as I have laid my forehead in your hands,
as I have drawn the warm breath
of your soul, wrapped in its redolence,

as I have heard you speak to me the words
the heart pours forth to show its mystery,
as I have seen, though weeping, yet seen smile,
your mouth on my mouth, your eye into mine,

as I have felt on my astonished head
the lightbeam of your star, still veiled,
while into the waters of my life one rose leaf
dropped out of the flurry of your days,

now I can say to the harrier of the years:
Go! I have nothing left to age! I'm done
with you and all your withered flowers.
I have here the flower none can cut!

Your wingstroke cannot shake from this cup
one drop of what fills it to the brim.
My soul has more fire than you have ashes!
My heart has more love than you have dark!

*Oceano nox*

Oh! combien de marins, combien de capitaines
Qui sont partis joyeux pour des courses lointaines,
Dans ce morne horizon se sont évanouis!
Combien ont disparu, dure et triste fortune!
Dans une mer sans fond, par une nuit sans lune,
Sous l'aveugle océan à jamais enfouis!

Combien de patrons morts avec leurs équipages!
L'ouragan de leur vie a pris toutes les pages
Et d'un souffle il a tout dispersé sur les flots!
Nul ne saura leur fin dans l'abîme plongée.
Chaque vague en passant d'un butin s'est chargée;
L'une a saisi l'esquif, l'autre les matelots!

Nul ne sait votre sort, pauvres têtes perdues!
Vous roulez à travers les sombres étendues,
Heurtant de vos fronts morts des écueils inconnus.
Oh! que de vieux parents, qui n'avaient plus qu'un rêve,
Sont morts en attendant tous les jours sur la grève
    Ceux qui ne sont pas revenus!

On s'entretient de vous parfois dans les veillées.
Maint joyeux cercle, assis sur des ancres rouillées,
Mêle encor quelque temps vos noms d'ombre couverts
Aux rires, aux refrains, aux récits d'aventures,
Aux baisers qu'on dérobe à vos belles futures,
Tandis que vous dormez dans les goémons verts!

On demande:—Où sont-ils? sont-ils rois dans quelque île?
Nous ont-ils délaissés pour un bord plus fertile?—
Puis votre souvenir même est enseveli.
Le corps se perd dans l'eau, le nom dans la mémoire.

*Oceano Nox*

How many captains, how many sailors,
glad to set off toward some distant port,
have vanished forever under this dark horizon!
How many went down with their luck
into the sea, under a night sky with no moon,
under a black wave, never to touch the earth again!

How many coxswains with their gear
have hurricanes thrown into the waves—like pages
torn from books unread!—the ends of them
secret in the abyss, breakers stealing away
downwind, each with its keepsakes, one
with the skiff, one with a dead man and an oar.

Nobody knows your fate, poor boys!—
who tumble under that dark expanse,
dead foreheads bumping into the hidden reefs.
Your families age with nothing to take your place
but thoughts. They die still looking out
    from shore for sons who never come!

We talk about you still, some nights,
a few of us, hunkering by the rusted anchor.
Your names console us after dark. We laugh,
we envy you your adventures, we remember
the kisses we stole from the girls who wanted you back,
while you slept under burgeoning rafts of kelp.

Somebody asks: Where are they? Are they kings
of islands somewhere? Have they left us
for a paradise on earth? Then, your names fade.
Bodies sink in the water, names in the mind.

Le temps, qui sur toute ombre en verse une plus noire,
Sur le sombre océan jette le sombre oubli.

Bientôt des yeux de tous votre ombre est disparue.
L'un n'a-t-il pas sa barque et l'autre sa charrue?
Seules, durant ces nuits où l'orage est vainqueur,
Vos veuves aux fronts blancs, lasses de vous attendre,
Parlent encor de vous en remuant la cendre
   De leur foyer et de leur cœur!

Et quand la tombe enfin a fermé leur paupière,
Rien ne sait plus vos noms, pas même une humble pierre
Dans l'étroit cimetière où l'écho nous répond,
Pas même un saule vert qui s'effeuille à l'automne,
Pas même la chanson naïve et monotone
Que chante un mendiant à l'angle d'un vieux pont!

Où sont-ils, les marins sombrés dans les nuits noires?
O flots, que vous savez de lugubres histoires!
Flots profonds redoutés des mères à genoux!
Vous vous les racontez en montant les marées,
Et c'est ce qui vous fait ces voix désespérées
Que vous avez le soir quand vous venez vers nous!

Time, dimming even the darkness, pours
oblivion into the nethermost gulf.

Soon from every eye your shadow fades.
One friend has a boat to keep, another a plow.
Alone, when the storms come after dark, your widows
pale from years of worry, now no longer fret
to speak of you, stirring·the embers on the grate,
    their memories like ash!

And after the coffins over their eyelids shut, no one
is left to say your name, not even a small stone
in the churchyard where the echoes visit,
not even a willow yellowing in the fall,
not even a simple, tuneless ballad
a beggar sings at the corner beside the bridge!

Where did they go, the sailors quenched in the dark?
Waves! what terrible stories you could tell
to the disbelieving mothers on their knees!
You keep repeating the details to yourself.
This is what makes the disconsolate voices
we hear crushing·into the rocks at night!

## Nuits de juin

L'été, lorsque le jour a fui, de fleurs couverte
La plaine verse au loin un parfum enivrant;
Les yeux fermés, l'oreille aux rumeurs entr'ouverte,
On ne dort qu'à demi d'un sommeil transparent.

Les astres sont plus purs, l'ombre paraît meilleure;
Un vague demi-jour teint le dôme éternel;
Et l'aube douce et pâle, en attendant son heure,
Semble toute la nuit errer au bas du ciel.

*28 septembre 1837.*

*Nights in June*

    Drunken summer, after the day ends, pours
the scent of wildflowers over the far-off meadow.
    Eyes closed, ears half open to murmurs,
sleep comes in the lucid dark of a trance.

    Stars more brilliant, darkness welcome,
twilight drifts off into the bowl of heaven,
    and glimmerings of sweet dawn to come
wander all night under the deep of the sky.

*L'Expiation*

I

Il neigeait. On était vaincu par sa conquête.
Pour la première fois l'aigle baissait la tête.
Sombres jours! l'empereur revenait lentement,
Laissant derrière lui brûler Moscou fumant.
Il neigeait. L'âpre hiver fondait en avalanche.
Après la plaine blanche une autre plaine blanche.
On ne connaissait plus les chefs ni le drapeau.
Hier la grande armée, et maintenant troupeau.
On ne distinguait plus les ailes ni le centre.
Il neigeait. Les blessés s'abritaient dans le ventre
Des chevaux morts; au seuil des bivouacs désolés
On voyait des clairons à leur poste gelés,
Restés debout, en selle et muets, blancs de givre,
Collant leur bouche en pierre aux trompettes de cuivre.
Boulets, mitraille, obus, mêlés aux flocons blancs,
Pleuvaient; les grenadiers, surpris d'être tremblants,
Marchaient pensifs, la glace à leur moustache grise.
Il neigeait, il neigeait toujours! La froide bise
Sifflait; sur le verglas, dans des lieux inconnus,
On n'avait pas de pain et l'on allait pieds nus.
Ce n'étaient plus des cœurs vivants, des gens de guerre:
C'était un rêve errant dans la brume, un mystère,
Une procession d'ombres sous le ciel noir.
La solitude vaste, épouvantable à voir,
Partout apparaissait, muette vengeresse.
Le ciel faisait sans bruit avec la neige épaisse
Pour cette immense armée un immense linceul.
Et chacun se sentant mourir, on était seul.
—Sortira-t-on jamais de ce funeste empire?
Deux ennemis! le czar, le nord. Le nord est pire.

*Napoleon's Army After the Fall of Moscow*

Snow, in what was left of the city behind them,
drifted into the smoke and flames.
In their retreat, the army did not know
one white field from another,
or the left flank from the right or center.
Ensigns whited out, the voices of commanders
lost, what had been an army was a herd.
More snow: mercury falling: some of the wounded
tried to shelter themselves
in the bellies of dead horses.
The bugler frozen to death at his post
stood upright, lips gone white with rime,
the brass of the trumpet locked
in the solid ice of his hand.
Flurries of riflefire blended with shrapnel
and snowflakes. The grenadier,
surprised to find himself now trembling,
marched with a more thoughtful step,
snot frozen in his mustache.
It snowed more still. The wind
out of the arctic sizzled; through strange country
slippery with pink ice, the barefoot soldiers
walked on without bread. These were not quite
living men, these wanderers in that fog:
they were a dream, a mystery,
a procession of shadows over a black sky.
Solitude settled into the mind of each,
like vengeance quietly gathering
out of the dreadful vastness. The sky made
turbid snow, over the largest army ever,

On jetait les canons pour brûler les aflûts.
Qui se couchait, mourait. Groupe morne et confus,
Ils fuyaient; le désert dévorait le cortège.
On pouvait, à des plis qui soulevaient la neige,
Voir que des régiments s'étaient endormis là.
O chutes d'Annibal! lendemains d'Attila!
Fuyards, blessés, mourants, caissons, brancards, civières,
On s'écrasait aux ponts pour passer les rivières,
On s'endormait dix mille, on se réveillait cent.
Ney, que suivait naguère une armée, à présent
S'évadait, disputant sa montre à trois cosaques.
Toutes les nuits, qui vive! alerte, assauts! attaques!
Ces fantômes prenaient leur fusil, et sur eux
Ils voyaient se ruer, effrayants, ténébreux,
Avec des cris pareils aux voix des vautours chauves,
D'horribles escadrons, tourbillons d'hommes fauves.
Toute une armée ainsi dans la nuit se perdait.
L'empereur était là, debout, qui regardait.
Il était comme un arbre en proie à la cognée.
Sur ce géant, grandeur jusqu'alors épargnée,
Le malheur, bûcheron sinistre, était monté;
Et lui, chêne vivant, par la hache insulté,
Tressaillant sous le spectre aux lugubres revanches,
Il regardait tomber autour de lui ses branches.
Chefs, soldats, tous mouraient. Chacun avait son tour.
Tandis qu'environnant sa tente avec amour,
Voyant son ombre aller et venir sur la toile,
Ceux qui restaient, croyant toujours à son étoile,
Accusaient le destin de lèse-majesté,
Lui se sentit soudain dans l'âme épouvanté.
Stupéfait du désastre et ne sachant que croire,
L'empereur se tourna vers Dieu; l'homme de gloire
Trembla; Napoléon comprit qu'il expiait
Quelque chose peut-être, et, livide, inquiet,
Devant ses légions sur la neige semées:
«Est-ce le châtiment, dit-il. Dieu des armées?»
Alors il s'entendit appeler par son nom
Et quelqu'un qui parlait dans l'ombre lui dit: Non.

an immeasurable shroud. Each of the soldiers fell
alone, struck by raiding troops,
or by the deadlier North.
They junked the cannon to burn the carriage.
Whoever slept for a moment died. The wasteland
swallowed them whole, regiments at a time,
visible now, where they lay down to rest,
as undulations in the anonymous snow.
Fugitives, wounded men, and dying,
in caissons, stretchers, and sleds, overloading
the bridges, falling asleep by the ten thousand,
woke up, hundreds, or less. A Duke
who weeks ago commanded obedience from battalions
pleaded with three Cossacks now to accept
his gold watch in exchange for bread.
Night after night, on the alert for attack,
dying soldiers took their rifles
and saw shadow squadrons come
from overhead like vultures flung down
screaming out of a whirlwind. Armies
died in a single night. The emperor,
before he fled, stood by, and watched,
and felt, as in the core of a great oak,
the clock of an inevitable ax.

*Mes deux filles*

Dans le frais clair-obscur du soir charmant qui tombe,
L'une pareille au cygne et l'autre à la colombe,
Belles, et toutes deux joyeuses, ô douceur!
Voyez, la grande sœur et la petite sœur
Sont assises au seuil du jardin, et sur elles
Un bouquet d'œillets blancs aux longues tiges frêles,
Dans une urne de marbre agité par le vent,
Se penche, et les regarde, immobile et vivant,
Et frissonne dans l'ombre, et semble, au bord du vase,
Un vol de papillons arrête dans l'extase.

*La Terrasse, près d'Enghien, juin 1842.*

*My Two Girls*

In the clear dark and the cool of evening,
one like a swan in her beauty, the other
a dove, and both of them happy: look!
Who could help smiling! Little sister,
and big, inside the garden gate on a low wall
where the tall white campions lean from the urn
as if to look more deeply into their faces,
vibrant even in stillness—the blossoms
spilling into the shadows, trembling in place,
like ecstasies of white moths frozen in flight.

Elle était déchaussée, elle était décoiffée,
Assise, les pieds nus, parmi les joncs penchants;
Moi qui passais par là, je crus voir une fée
Et je lui dis: Veux-tu t'en venir dans les champs?

Elle me regarda de ce regard suprême
Qui reste à la beauté quand nous en triomphons,
Et je lui dis: Veux-tu, c'est le mois où l'on aime,
Veux-tu nous en aller sous les arbres profonds?

Elle essuya ses pieds à l'herbe de la rive;
Elle me regarda pour la seconde fois,
Et la belle folâtre alors devint pensive.
Oh! comme les oiseaux chantaient au fond des bois!

Comme l'eau caressait doucement le rivage!
Je vis venir à moi, dans les grands roseaux verts,
La belle fille heureuse, effarée et sauvage,
Ses cheveux dans ses yeux, et riant au travers.

*Mont-l'Am., juin 183 . . .*

*Barefoot*

Her shoes pulled off, her hair let down,
she lay back under the leaning rushes, barefoot.
I stopped on the path, as if possessed, and said:
Would you like to walk with me into the fields?

She turned to me, supremely calm
as beauty is in its triumph, and I said:
If you like—it is the time of year for lovers—
we could walk under the trees. Would you like that?

She wiped her feet on the grass bank,
looking a second time in my face,
and frowning, pretending to be undecided.
Oh! how the birds sang in the deep woods!

The stream caressing its banks! And I watched her
step through the tall green rushes to meet me,
a young farmwoman, shy, and fierce, her hair
in her eyes, her cracked lips open, laughing.

## Lettre

Tu vois cela d'ici.—Des ocres et des craies,
Plaines où les sillons croisent leurs mille raies,
Chaumes à fleur de terre et que masque un buisson,
Quelques meules de foin debout sur le gazon,
De vieux toits enfumant le paysage bistre,
Un fleuve qui n'est pas le Gange ou le Caystre,
Pauvre cours d'eau normand troublé de sels marins,
A droite, vers le nord, de bizarres terrains
Pleins d'angles qu'on dirait façonnés à la pelle,
Voilà les premiers plans; une ancienne chapelle
Y mêle son aiguille, et range à ses côtés
Quelques ormes tortus, aux profils irrités,
Qui semblent, fatigués du zéphyr qui s'en joue,
Faire une remontrance au vent qui les secoue.
Une grosse charrette au coin de ma maison
Se rouille, et devant moi j'ai le vaste horizon
Dont la mer bleue emplit toutes les échancrures.
Des poules et des coqs, étalant leurs dorures,
Causent sous ma fenêtre, et les greniers des toits
Me jettent, par instants, des chansons en patois.
Dans mon allée habite un cordier patriarche,
Vieux qui fait bruyamment tourner sa roue, et marche
A reculons, son chanvre autour des reins tordu.
J'aime ces flots où court le grand vent éperdu;
Les champs à promener tout le jour me convient;
Les petits villageois, leur livre en main, m'envient,
Chez le maître d'école où je me suis logé,
Comme un grand écolier abusant d'un congé.
Le ciel rit, l'air est pur; tout le jour, chez mon hôte,
C'est un doux bruit d'enfants épelant à voix haute;
L'eau coule, un verdier passe: et, moi, je dis: Merci!
Merci, Dieu tout-puissant!—Ainsi je vis; ainsi,

*Letter from Normandy*

From here you see ten thousand streaks of chalk
and ocher where the furrows hatch the fields,
and half hid by the hedgerows, roofs thatched
almost to the ground, with woodsmoke from the chimneys
flattening around them in the hayricks and the stubble,
and the little river nearby that the tide makes
brackish. To the north is countryside as angular
as if it had been sculpted with a spade. This
is the foreground. Here an ancient steeple
rises over the wearied elms that sea winds
have been twisting into shape for centuries.
A big cart at the corner of my house is rusting,
and filling every notch hacked in a vast horizon
is the blue sea. Hens and roosters, showing off
their gilded feathers, gabble under my window,
and in the hayloft. Up the lane comes noise
of the old ropemaker at his wheel. I see him
lean back through his door with hemp cord cinched
around his hipbones. How I love this surf the wind
keeps breaking into a confused spray, and these
fields where I could walk forever! The children
going to school with books in hand watch me stride
out of the teacher's house, where I have lodgings,
into the open country, like a truant. The sky
laughs, the air is pure. Or, all day writing
in my room, I hear sweet voices from the children
at their lessons, mixed with flowing waters,
and a greenfinch singing. And my own voice says
out loud: Thanks be to God all-powerful for this!

Paisible, heure par heure, à petit bruit j'épanche
Mes jours, tout en songeant à vous, ma beauté blanche!
J'écoute les enfants jaser, et, par moment
Je vois en pleine mer passer superbement,
Au-dessus des pignons du tranquille village,
Quelque navire ailé qui fait un long voyage,
Et fuit sur l'océan, par tous les vents traqué,
Qui naguère dormait au port, le long du quai,
Et que n'ont retenu, loin des vagues jalouses,
Ni les pleurs des parents, ni l'effroi des épouses,
Ni le sombre reflet des écueils dans les eaux,
Ni l'importunité des sinistres oiseaux.

*Près le Tréport, juin 18*

These sights, these little sounds, this hour
overflowing into days of peace, where I can think
all day, no matter what, my darling, of your love!
Now, while the children chatter, under the gables
of the quiet village, onto the open sea, in superb
full sail, a great ship glides out on an oceanic
vastness beaten bright by winds from every quarter,
that same ship not long ago moored here
beside the quay, which cannot now be held back
from her voyage by landlocked jealousies,
or parents' tears, or fearfulness of spouses,
no, not even by the dark shapes of the reefs,
or by the importunings of prophetic seabirds.

*Souvenir de la nuit du 4*

L'enfant avait reçu deux balles dans la tête.
Le logis était propre, humble, paisible, honnête;
On voyait un rameau bénit sur un portrait.
Une vieille grand'mère était là qui pleurait.
Nous le déshabillions en silence. Sa bouche,
Pâle, s'ouvrait; la mort noyait son œil farouche;
Ses bras pendants semblaient demander des appuis.
Il avait dans sa poche une toupie en buis.
On pouvait mettre un doigt dans les trous de ses plaies.
Avez-vous vu saigner la mûre dans les haies?
Son crâne était ouvert comme un bois qui se fend.
L'aïeule regarda déshabiller l'enfant,
Disant:—Comme il est blanc! approchez donc la lampe.
Dieu! ses pauvres cheveux sont collés sur sa tempe!—
Et quand ce fut fini, le prit sur ses genoux.
La nuit était lugubre; on entendait des coups
De fusil dans la rue où l'on en tuait d'autres.
—Il faut ensevelir l'enfant, dirent les nôtres.
Et l'on prit un drap blanc dans l'armoire en noyer.
L'aïeule cependant l'approchait du foyer
Comme pour réchauffer ses membres déjà roides.
Hélas! ce que la mort touche de ses mains froides
Ne se réchauffe plus aux foyers d'ici-bas!
Elle pencha la tête et lui tira ses bas,
Et dans ses vieilles mains prit les pieds du cadavre.
—Est-ce que ce n'est pas une chose qui navre!
Cria-t-elle; monsieur, il n'avait pas huit ans!
Ses maîtres, il allait en classe, étaient contents.
Monsieur, quand il fallait que je fisse une lettre,
C'est lui qui l'écrivait. Est-ce qu'on va se mettre
A tuer les enfants maintenant? Ah! mon Dieu!

## How It Happened
   (December 4, 1851)

The boy had taken two shots in the head.
The apartment, though neat, was small,
with a crucifix over a family portrait.
His grandmother wept while we undressed him.
Speechless, his gray lips fell open. Death
had drowned out in his eye the last wild look.
His arms hung limp, as if they needed to be held.
He had in his pocket a boxwood top and string.
My forefinger would have fit in either wound.
Have you seen blackberries bleed? His skull
had been punched through easily as punkwood.
The old woman watched us strip him naked, saying:
He never looked this white! Bring me the lamp.
His hair, poor thing, it's stuck to his forehead.
With this she took him in her lap. The night
was an impossible depth of sadness. Rifles
in the street said, More now! You! Now you!
One of us inside said, Here, let's wrap the boy
in a sheet. And his grandmother carried him
to the fireside, as if his limbs
might still be warmed, even while invisible
cold hands went tight around them.
She lowered her head and pulled off his socks,
and took the corpse's feet in her cupped palms.
It breaks your heart, she said. Not
eight years old! His teachers gave him good
reports. And when I needed to send a letter,
he was the one who wrote it. So,
are they murdering children now? My God!

On est donc des brigands! Je vous demande un peu,
Il jouait ce matin, là, devant la fenêtre!
Dire qu'ils m'ont tué ce pauvre petit être!
Il passait dans la rue, ils ont tiré dessus.
Monsieur, il était bon et doux comme un Jésus.
Moi je suis vieille, il est tout simple que je parte;
Cela n'aurait rien fait à monsieur Bonaparte
De me tuer au lieu de tuer mon enfant!—
Elle s'interrompit, les sanglots l'étouffant,
Puis elle dit, et tous pleuraient près de l'aïeule:
—Que vais-je devenir à présent toute seule?
Expliquez-moi cela, vous autres, aujourd'hui.
Hélas! je n'avais plus de sa mère que lui.
Pourquoi l'a-t-on tué? je veux qu'on me l'explique.
L'enfant n'a pas crié vive la République.—

Nous nous taisions, debout et graves, chapeau bas,
Tremblant devant ce deuil qu'on ne console pas.

Vous ne compreniez point, mère, la politique.
Monsieur Napoléon, c'est son nom authentique,
Est pauvre, et même prince; il aime les palais;
Il lui convient d'avoir des chevaux, des valets,
De l'argent pour son jeu, sa table, son alcôve,
Ses chasses; par la même occasion, il sauve
La famille, l'église et la société;
Il veut avoir Saint-Cloud, plein de roses l'été,
Où viendront l'adorer les préfets et les maires;
C'est pour cela qu'il faut que les vieilles grand'mères,
De leurs pauvres doigts gris que fait trembler le temps,
Cousent dans le linceul des enfants de sept ans.

*2 décembre 1852. Jersey.*

Somebody tell me: are these people soldiers?
After breakfast, he was here at the window,
playing. This afternoon, he went walking
up that street, and they just shot him. Sir,
he was a good boy. He was sweet, like Jesus.
Me, I'm too old. It's past time for me to die.
It wouldn't be so bad: the President could send
his troops and have me shot down in the street,
but him, a little boy! Sobs choking her, she stopped,
and everyone was crying. Then she said,
And what becomes of me now, all alone? Can someone
tell me that? He was all I had left of his mother.
Why kill him? I need somebody to explain this for me.
This boy never had one thought about the President!

And everyone stood quiet, shaken
by this grief that no one ever would console.

But let me say, old woman, to make clear
what you have missed: Napoleon, though poor, is
still a prince, and he loves palaces. A prince
needs horses, household help, and money,
for the pastimes of a princely table, for the boudoir,
and the hunt. Of course, he must preserve the family
too, society, the church, and so on, not to mention
such prime real estate as Saint-Cloud,
where great men among the summer roses act
as worshipful as one is rich. On this account,
a few old women with arthritic fingers must
stitch winding sheets around their little boys.

Elle avait pris ce pli dans son âge enfantin
De venir dans ma chambre un peu chaque matin;
Je l'attendais ainsi qu'un rayon qu'on espère;
Elle entrait, et disait: Bonjour, mon petit père;
Prenait ma plume, ouvrait mes livres, s'asseyait
Sur mon lit, dérangeait mes papiers, et riait,
Puis soudain s'en allait comme un oiseau qui passe.
Alors, je reprenais, la tête un peu moins lasse,
Mon œuvre interrompue, et, tout en écrivant,
Parmi mes manuscrits je rencontrais souvent
Quelque arabesque folle et qu'elle avait tracée,
Et mainte page blanche entre ses mains froissée
Où, je ne sais comment, venaient mes plus doux vers.
Elle aimait Dieu, les fleurs, les astres, les prés verts,
Et c'était un esprit avant d'être une femme.
Son regard reflétait la clarté de son âme.
Elle me consultait sur tout à tous moments.
Oh! que de soirs d'hiver radieux et charmants
Passés à raisonner langue, histoire et grammaire,
Mes quatre enfants groupés sur mes genoux, leur mère
Tout près, quelques amis causant au coin du feu!
J'appelais cette vie être content de peu!
Et dire qu'elle est morte! Hélas! que Dieu m'assiste!
Je n'étais jamais gai quand je la sentais triste;
J'étais morne au milieu du bal le plus joyeux
Si j'avais, en partant, vu quelque ombre en ses yeux.

*Novembre 1846, jour des morts.*

## *All Souls' Day, 1846*

At four years old, first thing when she woke up,
she visited my room, and I would wait,
as hopeful as for sunlight. She came in
and said: Good morning, sweet Papa!
and took my quill, flipped the pages
of my books, sat on my bed, scattered
my papers, laughed—and she was gone
more quickly than a greenfinch at the window.
Then, I turned back to my work less drained,
and, lost again in writing, I would find
somewhere she scribbled, say, an arabesque,
or I might find a blank page crumpled
by her hands, which, strangely, would release
her tenderness into my poems, the best of them.
She loved God, flowers, stars, green meadows,
with a child's mind ready to unfold into a woman,
her least look reflecting light clear from her soul.
She would ask me things, and we would pass
a winter's night in pleasant study, talking
history and language, my four children gathered
at my chair, their mother near, a few friends chatting
by the fireside. She made me think, to be content
with little was my nature. Then, she died,
which left me blaming God, and asking Him for help.
I never could be happy when I thought her sad.
I brooded one night through the most delightful party
having, on our way out, seen her with a gloomy look.

Quand nous habitions tous ensemble
Sur nos collines d'autrefois,
Où l'eau court, où le buisson tremble,
Dans la maison qui touche aux bois,

Elle avait dix ans, et moi trente;
J'étais pour elle l'univers.
Oh! comme l'herbe est odorante
Sous les arbres profonds et verts!

Elle faisait mon sort prospère,
Mon travail léger, mon ciel bleu.
Lorsqu'elle me disait: Mon père,
Tout mon cœur s'écriait: Mon Dieu!

A travers mes songes sans nombre,
J'écoutais son parler joyeux,
Et mon front s'éclairait dans l'ombre
A la lumière de ses yeux.

Elle avait l'air d'une princesse
Quand je la tenais par la main.
Elle cherchait des fleurs sans cesse
Et des pauvres dans le chemin.

Elle donnait comme on dérobe,
En se cachant aux yeux de tous.
Oh! la belle petite robe
Qu'elle avait, vous rappelez-vous?

*When We Were Living*
  (September 4, 1844)


When we were living, all of us,
under the hill where the river spoke,
where the rosebush shook, and the house
in innocence touched the woods,

she was ten, and I was thirty.
I was her world! and she was mine!
How the scent of the grass grows
sweet under the dark green trees!

She made good luck of my life,
all of it swept up in the blue,
and when she said, Papa! I felt
God tremble in the word.

Sometimes in my dreams
I could hear her idle talk,
and my face shone in the dark
with a glimmering from her eyes.

She would be the one to lead me
when I took her hand.
We looked everywhere for flowers,
meeting the poor at the wayside:

she gave gifts the way some steal,
in secret, for the thrill.
Oh! and that little frock
she wore, do you remember?

Le soir, auprès de ma bougie,
Elle jasait à petit bruit,
Tandis qu'à la vitre rougie
Heurtaient les papillons de nuit.

Les anges se miraient en elle.
Que son bonjour était charmant!
Le ciel mettait dans sa prunelle
Ce regard qui jamais ne ment.

Oh! je l'avais, si jeune encore,
Vue apparaître en mon destin!
C'était l'enfant de mon aurore,
Et mon étoile du matin!

Quand la lune claire et sereine
Brillait aux cieux, dans ces beaux mois
Comme nous allions dans la plaine!
Comme nous courions dans les bois!

Puis, vers la lumière isolée
Etoilant le logis obscur,
Nous revenions par la vallée
En tournant le coin du vieux mur;

Nous revenions, cœurs pleins de flamme,
En parlant des splendeurs du ciel.
Je composais cette jeune âme
Comme l'abeille fait son miel.

Doux ange aux candides pensées,
Elle était gaie en arrivant . . . —
Toutes ces choses sont passées
Comme l'ombre et comme le vent!

                  *Villequier, 4 septembre 1844.*

Evenings by my study lamp,
she made up a silly song
while moths tapped
into the windowpane.

Angels admired themselves in her,
the way her happiness gave joy!
And what was true her eyes
reflected, like the sky.

I could see my destiny
made sweet in her approach!
She was my dawn,
my morning star!

And nights when the full moon
soared, the two of us walked out
through silver fields and ran
far into the quiet woods!

Then, toward the single lamp
that burned in the dark house,
we came back along the river
past the turn of an ancient wall.

We came back, our hearts one flame,
saying aloud the names of stars,
to feed our souls on heaven,
the way bees do with honey.

Angel, sweet with her frank thoughts,
happy wherever she went, now
everything she gave is gone.
The past is shadows in the wind.

Demain, dès l'aube, à l'heure où blanchit la campagne,
Je partirai. Vois-tu, je sais que tu m'attends.
J'irai par la forêt, j'irai par la montagne.
Je ne puis demeurer loin de toi plus longtemps.

Je marcherai les yeux fixés sur mes pensées,
Sans rien voir au dehors, sans entendre aucun bruit,
Seul, inconnu, le dos courbé, les mains croisées,
Triste, et le jour pour moi sera comme la nuit.

Je ne regarderai ni l'or du soir qui tombe,
Ni les voiles au loin descendant vers Harfleur,
Et quand j'arriverai, je mettrai sur ta tombe
Un bouquet de houx vert et de bruyère en fleur.

*3 septembre 1847.*

*Little Song*
   (to Leopoldine, September 3, 1847)


Tomorrow, with dawn's whitewash on the fields,
I will leave. I can feel you waiting. Wait!
I shall walk through the woods and mountains.
I cannot stay away from you here any longer.

Eyes fixed into thought, though I walk,
I see nothing outside, I hear not a sound,
a strange old man hunched over my folded hands.
Day to my mind is a sad stain on the darkness.

I shall not look into the golden evening,
or at the sails in the distance raising Harfleur,
and when I arrive, I shall lay on your gravestone
twigs of green holly and heather picked in full flower.

*A Villequier*

Maintenant que Paris, ses pavés et ses marbres,
Et sa brume et ses toits sont bien loin de mes yeux;
Maintenant que je suis sous les branches des arbres,
Et que je puis songer à la beauté des cieux;

Maintenant que du deuil qui m'a fait l'âme obscure
　　Je sors, pâle et vainqueur,
Et que je sens la paix de la grande nature
　　Qui m'entre dans le cœur;

Maintenant que je puis, assis au bord des ondes,
Emu par ce superbe et tranquille horizon,
Examiner en moi les vérités profondes
Et regarder les fleurs qui sont dans le gazon;

Maintenant, ô mon Dieu! que j'ai ce calme sombre
　　De pouvoir désormais
Voir de mes yeux la pierre où je sais que dans l'ombre
　　Elle dort pour jamais;

Maintenant qu'attendri par ces divins spectacles,
Plaines, forêts, rochers, vallons, fleuve argenté,
Voyant ma petitesse et voyant vos miracles,
Je reprends ma raison devant l'immensité;

Je viens à vous, Seigneur, père auquel il faut croire;
　　Je vous porte, apaisé,
Les morceaux de ce cœur tout plein de votre gloire
　　Que voux avez brisé;

*The Graveyard at Villequier*
  (September 4, 1847)


Now, with the streets of Paris and the stones,
the haze and roofs, all out of sight,
now, under the branching trees,
under the dreaming brilliance of the sky,

now, out of the darkness, after the years spent mourning,
    ghastly here in my triumph,
now that I come to feel the peace of universal nature
    breaking into my heart;

now that I can sit beside the waves, in awe
of oceanic splendor calm to the horizon;
now that I look inside myself at distant truths
and see the little flowers near me in the grass;

now, my Lord, that I can feel your silent power, able,
    as day fades, with unafflicted eyes
at last to see the stone where in the shade
    I know she sleeps forever;

now left tender, Lord, by this vast show of yours,
the plains, the woods and crags, the valley
with its river lit white gold, seeing my smallness:
I regain my reason here in view of your immensity.

I come to you, my Father, who requires my faith.
    I bring you, quieted,
the tribute of this heart suffused with glory, torn
    to pieces by your will.

Je viens à vous, Seigneur! confessant que vous êtes
Bon, clément, indulgent et doux, ô Dieu vivant!
Je conviens que vous seul savez ce que vous faites,
Et que l'homme n'est rien qu'un jonc qui tremble au vent;

Je dis que le tombeau qui sur les morts se ferme
    Ouvre le firmament;
Et que ce qu'ici-bas nous prenons pour le terme
    Est le commencement;

Je conviens à genoux que vous seul, père auguste,
Possédez l'infini, le réel, l'absolu;
Je conviens qu'il est bon, je conviens qu'il est juste
Que mon cœur ait saigné, puisque Dieu l'a voulu!

Je ne résiste plus à tout ce qui m'arrive
    Par votre volonté.
L'âme de deuils en deuils, l'homme de rive en rive,
    Roule à l'éternité.

Nous ne voyons jamais qu'un seul côté des choses;
L'autre plonge en la nuit d'un mystère effrayant.
L'homme subit le joug sans connaître les causes.
Tout ce qu'il voit est court, inutile et fuyant.

Vous faites revenir toujours la solitude
    Autour de tous ses pas.
Vous n'avez pas voulu qu'il eût la certitude
    Ni la joie ici-bas!

Dès qu'il possède un bien, le sort le lui retire.
Rien ne lui fut donné, dans ses rapides jours,
Pour qu'il s'en puisse faire une demeure, et dire:
C'est ici ma maison, mon champ et mes amours!

Il doit voir peu de temps tout ce que ses yeux voient;
    Il vieillit sans soutiens.

I come to you, my Lord! confessing, you alone
are merciful and sweet, o living God! I now admit
that your mind only can encompass what you do.
A man is nothing but a stem vibrating in the wind.

I say, the tomb which we see closing on the dead
   is opening into the sky.
What hereabouts we take to be the end
   is elsewhere the beginning.

I admit now on my knees that you alone, dear Father,
keep the infinite, the real, the absolute.
I grant, because God willed that my heart bleed,
this must be good. I grant my pain is just.

What hurts me by God's will now I resist
   no more. The soul
from grief to grief, from shore to shore,
   keeps rocking endlessly.

The world we see is just this side. The other
plunges us in an unfathomable night. A man
bends to the yoke, never knowing the cause,
and all he sees is brief and useless.

You, God, keep his every step in this world
   fraught with solitude.
You have not wanted him to know the steadiness
   of truth or joy.

Whatever good he knows, fate takes it—
nothing in this life will stand for him
to call a dwelling place, for him to say:
Here, this is home, this field, these loves.

What his eyes can see at all is flickering.
   He ages, stooped, without support.

Puisque ces choses sont, c'est qu'il faut qu'elles soient;
   J'en conviens, j'en conviens!

Le monde est sombre, ô Dieu! l'immuable harmonie
Se compose des pleurs aussi bien que des chants;
L'homme n'est qu'un atome en cette ombre infinie,
Nuit où montent les bons, où tombent les méchants.

Je sais que vous avez bien autre chose à faire
   Que de nous plaindre tous,
Et qu'un enfant qui meurt, désespoir de sa mère,
   Ne vous fait rien, à vous!

Je sais que le fruit tombe au vent qui le secoue,
Que l'oiseau perd sa plume et la fleur son parfum;
Que la création est une grande roue
Qui ne peut se mouvoir sans écraser quelqu'un;

Les mois, les jours, les flots des mers, les yeux qui pleurent,
   Passent sous le ciel bleu;
Il faut que l'herbe pousse et que les enfants meurent;
   Je le sais, ô mon Dieu!

Dans vos cieux, au delà de la sphère des nues,
Au fond de cet azur immobile et dormant,
Peut-être faites-vous des choses inconnues
Où la douleur de l'homme entre comme élément.

Peut-être est-il utile à vos desseins sans nombre
   Que des êtres charmants
S'en aillent, emportés par le tourbillon sombre
   Des noirs événements.

Nos destins ténébreux vont sous des lois immenses
Que rien ne déconcerte et que rien n'attendrit.
Vous ne pouvez avoir de subites clémences
Qui dérangent le monde, ô Dieu, tranquille esprit!

And as things are, so must they be. All this
   I grant, Dear God, all this!

The world is dark. Its unrelenting harmony
includes as well as hymns the cries
of human atoms in an endless dark where things,
both good and evil, rise and fall.

I know, you have much else to do besides
   take pity on our lot.
A child who dies, who leaves her mother in despair,
   to you means nothing.

This I know, fruit falls into the wind that jolts it.
The bird loses her feather, the flower her scent.
Your whole creation is a vast wheel
which to turn at all must crush someone.

A month, a day, a tide, a tear on a human face,
   all fade under the blue sky.
Grass must sprout and children drown—
   I know this well, my Lord!

Beyond this clouded sphere, beyond these skies
of motionless, unthinking azure, maybe
you have fashioned some great mystery
where human sorrows enter as an element,

where in some incalculable plan it serves
   that certain joyful creatures
be swept under into the darkening whirlpool
   of what happens by your will.

Your dark designs entail immensities of law
that nothing disconcerts or mollifies.
You cannot entertain the whims of mercy
and upset the world. Your mind is imperturbable.

Je vous supplie, ô Dieu! de regarder mon âme,
   Et de considérer
Qu'humble comme un enfant et doux comme une femme,
   Je viens vous adorer!

Considérez encor que j'avais, dès l'aurore,
Travaillé, combattu, pensé, marché, lutté,
Expliquant la nature à l'homme qui l'ignore,
Eclairant toute chose avec votre clarté;

Que j'avais, affrontant la haine et la colère,
   Fait ma tâche ici-bas,
Que je ne pouvais pas m'attendre à ce salaire,
   Que je ne pouvais pas

Prévoir que, vous aussi, sur ma tête qui ploie
Vous appesantiriez votre bras triomphant,
Et que, vous qui voyiez comme j'ai peu de joie,
Vous me reprendriez si vite mon enfant!

Qu'une âme ainsi frappée à se plaindre est sujette,
   Que j'ai pu blasphémer,
Et vous jeter mes cris comme un enfant qui jette
   Une pierre à la mer!

Considérez qu'on doute, ô mon Dieu! quand on souffre,
Que l'œil qui pleure trop finit par s'aveugler,
Qu'un être que son deuil plonge au plus noir du gouffre,
Quand il ne vous voit plus, ne peut vous contempler,

Et qu'il ne se peut pas que l'homme, lorsqu'il sombre
   Dans les afflictions,
Ait présente à l'esprit la sérénité sombre
   Des constellations!

Aujourd'hui, moi qui fus faible comme une mère,
Je me courbe à vos pieds devant vos cieux ouverts.

I pray, my God, that you regard my soul
   and see how,
humble as a child and tender as a woman,
   I now come to you in praise!

See, again, how I have worked since dawn, again
done battle, thought, pressed forward, striven
to make known to men the truths of nature,
showing each thing clearly in your light.

See, though met by hatred, faced with anger,
   having done my work on earth,
how I could not foresee such payment in return,
   how I had never guessed

you too would let the whole weight of your arm
come down in its omnipotence onto a head
so bowed, and, seeing that I had so little
joy, that you would take my child!

Consider how a soul thus beaten might complain,
   how I might blaspheme,
throwing you my curse the way a boy would throw
   a stone into the ocean.

Consider how, in doubt, my Lord, in suffering,
with eyes too full of tears, gone blind, plunged
into the blackest depth of grief, in sight of nothing,
wracked, a mind might lose it blessedness,

and how it cannot be that under the dark
   of such affliction
consciousness would apprehend as your serene
   display the stars!

Yet now, made weak by love as any mother,
I bow down beneath your feet under the twilight,

Je me sens éclairé dans ma douleur amère
Par un meilleur regard jeté sur l'univers.

Seigneur, je reconnais que l'homme est en délire
    S'il ose murmurer;
Je cesse d'accuser, je cesse de maudire,
    Mais laissez-moi pleurer!

Hélas! laissez les pleurs couler de ma paupière,
Puisque vous avez fait les hommes pour cela!
Laissez-moi me pencher sur cette froide pierre
Et dire à mon enfant: Sens-tu que je suis là?

Laissez-moi lui parler, incliné sur ses restes,
    Le soir, quand tout se tait,
Comme si, dans sa nuit rouvrant ses yeux célestes,
    Cet ange m'écoutait!

Hélas! vers le passé tournant un œil d'envie,
Sans que rien ici-bas puisse m'en consoler,
Je regarde toujours ce moment de ma vie
Où je l'ai vue ouvrir son aile et s'envoler!

Je verrai cet instant jusqu'à ce que je meure,
    L'instant, pleurs superflus!
Où je criai: L'enfant que j'avais tout à l'heure,
    Quoi donc! je ne l'ai plus!

Ne vous irritez pas que je sois de la sorte,
O mon Dieu! cette plaie a si longtemps saigné!
L'angoisse dans mon âme est toujours la plus forte,
Et mon cœur est soumis, mais n'est pas résigné.

Ne vous irritez pas! fronts que le deuil réclame,
    Mortels sujets aux pleurs,
Il nous est malaisé de retirer notre âme
    De ces grandes douleurs.

feeling, as I cast a clearer look
into the universe, the clearing of my grief.

My God, I understand it, that the man is mad
    who dares object.
I quit accusing you. I quit the cursing.
    Please, though, let me cry!

At least let tears still blur my sight,
since you designed the flesh for this!
Just let me lean against this stone and ask
my child if she can feel that I am here.

Just let me talk to her, what's left of her
    this evening in this hush,
as if in her unending night her eyes came open
    and she heard me!

Still, I turn back to the past with yearnings
that no consummation in this world can ever soothe,
and always I look toward that moment
when I saw her lift her wing and she was gone.

I see her still, and shall until I die relive
    that moment overflowing tears
when I cried: Look! The child I had just now
    I have no more!

You, Lord, must not be angry that I am so
minded, when this wound has bled so long!
Anguish always is the greater portion of my soul.
My heart submits, but I am not resigned.

Forgive me, also, you whom grief has made
    like me the source of tears.
It takes such strength to drag the soul up
    from that aching depth.

Voyez-vous, nos enfants nous sont bien nécessaires,
Seigneur; quand on a vu dans sa vie, un matin,
Au milieu des ennuis, des peines, des misères,
Et de l'ombre que fait sur nous notre destin,

Apparaître un enfant, tête chère et sacrée,
　　Petit être joyeux,
Si beau, qu'on a cru voir s'ouvrir à son entrée
　　Une porte des cieux;

Quand on a vu, seize ans, de cet autre soi-même
Croître la grâce aimable et la douce raison,
Lorsqu'on a reconnu que cet enfant qu'on aime
Fait le jour dans notre âme et dans notre maison,

Que c'est la seule joie ici-bas qui persiste
　　De tout ce qu'on rêva,
Considérez que c'est une chose bien triste
　　De le voir qui s'en va!

Look here! We need our children, God.
To see one morning in this life
of boredom, in our misery and pain,
under the shadow fate lets fall on us,

a child's dear head, the blessedness
    of this small joy,
this sight so lovely it could be the opening
    of a passway into heaven,

and to see, for nineteen years, this other self
increase in loving kindness, in sweet reason,
till the child has brought into the soul
that loves her and the house they share

the light that is the only lasting joy on earth
    of any ever to be known,
consider what a sad thing, then,
    to see her go.

*Paroles sur la dune*

Maintenant que mon temps décroît comme un flambeau,
   Que mes tâches sont terminées;
Maintenant que voici que je touche au tombeau
   Par les deuils et par les années,

Et qu'au fond de ce ciel que mon essor rêva,
   Je vois fuir, vers l'ombre entraînées,
Comme le tourbillon du passé qui s'en va,
   Tant de belles heures sonnées;

Maintenant que je dis:—Un jour, nous triomphons;
   Le lendemain, tout est mensonge!—
Je suis triste, et je marche au bord des flots profonds,
   Courbé comme celui qui songe.

Je regarde, au-dessus du mont et du vallon,
   Et des mers sans fin remuées,
S'envoler, sous le bec du vautour aquilon,
   Toute la toison des nuées;

J'entends le vent dans l'air, la mer sur le récif,
   L'homme liant la gerbe mûre;
J'écoute, et je confronte en mon esprit pensif
   Ce qui parle à ce qui murmure;

Et je reste parfois couché sans me lever
   Sur l'herbe rare de la dune,
Jusqu'à l'heure où l'on voit apparaître et rêver
   Les yeux sinistres de la lune.

*Word from the Dunes*
   (August 5, 1854, the second anniversary of the poet's
   exile on the island of Jersey)


Now that my lamp burns lower,
   now that my task is ended,
here where the griefs and years have carried me
   almost into the grave,

while my thoughts veer deeper into a darkening sky,
   I can see the hour of good fortune,
on the whirlwind of the past borne
   into the darkness, disappear.

Now I declare, the day of triumph proves,
   the following day, a lie.
I walk at the edge of the great waves, sad,
   a man bent double by unwieldy dreams.

And over the mountains and the lowlands,
   over the high waves,
I can see the gale with a vulture's beak tear
   into the fleece of driven clouds.

I hear the wind snap into the air, the sea on the reef,
   the farmers binding their ripe grain,
and I listen, measuring in my pensiveness
   what speaks against what moans.

I stay for a long time without moving, prone
   on the scant grass of the dunes,
until the eyes of the moon appear to me
   like a bad omen in a dream,

Elle monte, elle jette un long rayon dormant
    A l'espace, au mystère, au gouffre;
Et nous nous regardons tous les deux fixement,
    Elle qui brille et moi qui souffre.

Où donc s'en sont allés mes jours évanouis?
    Est-il quelqu'un qui me connaisse?
Ai-je encor quelque chose en mes yeux éblouis,
    De la clarté de ma jeunesse?

Tout s'est-il envolé? Je suis seul, je suis las;
    J'appelle sans qu'on me réponde;
O vents! ô flots! ne suis-je aussi qu'un souffle, hélas!
    Hélas! ne suis-je aussi qu'une onde?

Ne verrai-je plus rien de tout ce que j'aimais?
    Au dedans de moi le soir tombe.
O terre, dont la brume efface les sommets,
    Suis-je le spectre, et toi la tombe?

Ai-je donc vidé tout, vie, amour, joie, espoir?
    J'attends, je demande, j'implore;
Je penche tour à tour mes urnes pour avoir
    De chacune une goutte encore!

Comme le souvenir est voisin du remord!
    Comme à pleurer tout nous ramène!
Et que je te sens froide en te touchant, ô mort,
    Noir verrou de la porte humaine!

Et je pense, écoutant gémir le vent amer,
    Et l'onde aux plis infranchissables;
L'été rit, et l'on voit sur le bord de la mer
    Fleurir le chardon bleu des sables.

        *5 août 1854, anniversaire de mon arrivée à Jersey.*

rising, sending a long dull ray into the emptiness,
    into the mystery, the abyss—
the two of us, our gazes fixed, the glamorous
    moon and I who grieve.

What's to become of the vanishing days?
    Can anyone see the man I was?
Is there in my bedazzled eyes still anything
    of the gleam of youth?

Or am I now alone, worn out, merely to ask,
    where nothing answers:
Wind, am I not like you a breath? Waves,
    do I not break like you?

And shall I see no more of what I loved?
    Night inside me falls. So,
tell me, World, dissolving at your edges into mist,
    am I the ghost and you the grave?

Have I now spent my life—my love and joy
    and hope? Is nothing left?
I plead, and tip the urns, to try them
    one by one for another drop!

But memory is itself remorse! And every thought
    returns the mind to tears!
While everything I feel is cool with death and solid
    as a black bolt on the door!

Listening to a bitter wind, I see waves lift
    insuperable coils, and on the dunes
the summer, brilliant as a stranger's laugh, upholds
    another flowering of blue thistle.

*Nomen, numen, lumen*

Quand il eut terminé, quand les soleils épars,
Eblouis, du chaos montant de toutes parts,
Se furent tous rangés à leur place profonde,
Il sentit le besoin de se nommer au monde;
Et l'être formidable et serein se leva;
Il se dressa sur l'ombre et cria: JÉHOVAH!
Et dans l'immensité ces sept lettres tombèrent;
Et ce sont, dans les cieux que nos yeux réverbèrent,
Au-dessus de nos fronts tremblants sous leur rayon,
Les sept astres géants du noir septentrion.

*The Seven Oxen of the Northern Plough*

When he had done, when the disheveled,
dazzling stars spun out of chaos
into their places in the dark, he felt
the need to name himself to the world,
and awful, yet serene, he let his being
rise up out of the dark to cry: JEHOVAH!
the seven letters soaring into the night sky
so that our trembling foreheads feel them still
in the seven beams of the black septentrion.

*Pasteurs et troupeaux*

Le vallon où je vais tous les jours est charmant,
Serein, abandonné, seul sous le firmament,
Plein de ronces en fleurs; c'est un sourire triste.
Il vous fait oublier que quelque chose existe,
Et, sans le bruit des champs remplis de travailleurs,
On ne saurait plus là si quelqu'un vit ailleurs.
Là, l'ombre fait l'amour; l'idylle naturelle
Rit; le bouvreuil avec le verdier s'y querelle.
Et la fauvette y met de travers son bonnet;
C'est tantôt l'aubépine et tantôt le genêt;
De noirs granits bourrus, puis des mousses riantes;
Car Dieu fait un poème avec des variantes;
Comme le vieil Homère, il rabâche parfois,
Mais c'est avec les fleurs, les monts, l'onde et les bois!
Une petite mare est là, ridant sa face,
Prenant des airs de flot pour la fourmi qui passe,
Ironie étalée au milieu du gazon,
Qu'ignore l'océan grondant à l'horizon.
J'y rencontre parfois sur la roche hideuse
Un doux être; quinze ans, yeux bleus, pieds nus, gardeuse
De chèvres, habitant, au fond d'un ravin noir,
Un vieux chaume croulant qui s'étoile le soir;
Ses sœurs sont au logis et filent leur quenouille;
Elle essuie aux roseaux ses pieds que l'étang mouille;
Chèvres, brebis, béliers, paissent; quand, sombre esprit,
J'apparais, le pauvre ange a peur, et me sourit;
Et moi, je la salue, elle étant l'innocence.
Ses agneaux, dans le pré plein de fleurs qui l'encense,
Bondissent, et chacun, au soleil s'empourprant,
Laisse aux buissons, à qui la bise le reprend,
Un peu de sa toison, comme un flocon d'écume.
Je passe; enfant, troupeau, s'effacent dans la brume;

## Shepherds and Flocks

The valley where I walk most days looks, though abandoned,
calm, as if content under the vast sky in its loneliness,
with blackberry bushes in flower, like a sad smile making
a man forget what else if anything exists. Out of earshot
of the workers in the fields nearby, who could tell
from here if any world but this were still alive!
A shadow soothes me like a lover's hand. The bullfinch
and the greenfinch wrangle. The warbler, barking,
tips his head. Hawthorne and broom flowers open.
Under the edges of black granite soft with mosses
God has made a poem with variations, often like old Homer
repeating himself, but in God's case with wildflowers,
hillsides, streams, and woods! That little pond there
wrinkling (I would say, with inner cheerfulness)
into a kind of smile, looms like a vast flood
over the ant, oblivious in the thick of the grass
to the Atlantic roaring on the horizon. I see here
sometimes on a monstrous rock a girl about fifteen,
with blue eyes, barefoot, tending her goats. She lives
at the floor of a dark ravine, under a sagging thatch
with gaps where stars shine through. Her sisters
stay home days to spin the mohair. Now she wipes
her muddy feet clean on the rushes. Goats, and ewes
and rams, graze. Gloomy apparition that I am, alas,
she fears me, but she smiles, and I bid her my best
good day, she being innocent. Her lambs, in a field
of flowers that incense them, buck and skitter, each
in the briars under the purpled sun leaving a little
of its fleece to shine in the dry gust like a tuft of foam.
I go. The child, her flock, lost to me in the mist.

Le crépuscule étend sur les longs sillons gris
Ses ailes de fantôme et de chauve-souris;
J'entends encore au loin dans la plaine ouvrière
Chanter derrière moi la douce chevrière,
Et, là-bas, devant moi, le vieux gardien pensif
De l'écume, du flot, de l'algue, du récif,
Et des vagues sans trêve et sans fin remuées,
Le pâtre promontoire au chapeau de nuées,
S'accoude et rêve au bruit de tous les infinis,
Et, dans l'ascension des nuages bénis,
Regarde se lever la lune triomphale,
Pendant que l'ombre tremble, et que l'âpre rafale
Disperse à tous les vents avec son souffle amer
La laine des moutons sinistres de la mer.

*Jersey, Grouville, avril 1855.*

Twilight spreads in the long gray furrows softly
under the wings of phantom bats. Still I can hear,
over the open fields behind me, that sweet song
the goat girl sings going home. Far ahead, over the mists,
over the tides and seaweed, reefs, and waves oncoming
without respite, with no end, her ancient guardian,
the headland, brooding under a herdsman's cap of clouds,
leans like a god on his elbow and dreams into the tumult
of infinity, while watching in the ascension of the clouds
this triumphal moonrise, under which the dark
is trembling, and the squall bears down to scatter
on bleak winds the wool of the deadly flock of the sea.

*Mugitusque boum*

Mugissement des bœufs, au temps du doux Virgile,
Comme aujourd'hui, le soir, quand fuit la nue agile,
Ou, le matin, quand l'aube aux champs extasiés
Verse à flots la rosée et le jour, vous disiez:

—Mûrissez, blés mouvants! prés, emplissez-vous d'herbes!
Que la terre, agitant son panache de gerbes,
Chante dans l'onde d'or d'une riche moisson!
Vis, bête; vis, caillou; vis, homme; vis, buisson!
A l'heure où le soleil se couche, où l'herbe est pleine
Des grands fantômes noirs des arbres de la plaine
Jusqu'aux lointains coteaux rampant et grandissant,
Quand le brun laboureur des collines descend
Et retourne à son toit d'où sort une fumée,
Que la soif de revoir sa femme bien-aimée
Et l'enfant qu'en ses bras hier il réchauffait,
Que ce désir, croissant à chaque pas qu'il fait,
Imite dans son cœur l'allongement de l'ombre!
Etres! choses! vivez! sans peur, sans deuil, sans nombre!
Que tout s'épanouisse en sourire vermeil!
Que l'homme ait le repos et la bœuf le sommeil!
Vivez! croissez! semez le grain à l'aventure!
Qu'on sente frissonner dans toute la nature,
Sous la feuille des nids, au seuil blanc des maisons,
Dans l'obscur tremblement des profonds horizons,
Un vaste emportement d'aimer, dans l'herbe verte,
Dans l'antre, dans l'étang, dans la clairière ouverte,
D'aimer sans fin, d'aimer toujours, d'aimer encor,
Sous la sérénité des sombres astres d'or!
Faites tressaillir l'air, le flot, l'aile, la bouche,
O palpitations du grand amour farouche!

## Mugitusque Boum

Lowing of cattle: your voice, to the mind of Virgil,
felt mellifluous, as it does this evening
when a cloud slips off into the dark of the sky,
or as when dawn on the transfixing fields
pours dew in streams and daylight. You say:

Ripen, wheatfields under the wind! Hayfields
flourish! Let earth, waving its green plume
over the meadow, sing in the brookwater
of a golden harvest! Live, you fellow beasts! you,
bushes, even gravel crunched by hooves, and you too,
herdsmen, live! Let sunset pour across the field
the trees of shadow that rear up onto the far slope,
huge, where farmers come down from the mountain,
tanned, toward woodsmoke rising from farmhouses,
thirsty, longing for the sight of wives and children,
for the warmth of them in arms that ache with clearing
stone from pasture. Let the desire, increased in them
with each step, overflow the expanded shadows.
Things and creatures, live! Be unafraid, unmournful.
Everywhere, let bloom with crimson life! Let men
rest! Let us cattle sleep! But live, you sowers,
cast the grain at random! Let the thrill of being
sing through all things, into the feathered nest,
over the white stone threshold, deep into the trembling
of an obscure vastness. May the potent urge to love
enter the green shoot, cave, and pond, and clearing,
love without end, love forever, and beyond that
love, under the calm of sombered golden stars.
Yet startle! air, and flood, and wing, and mouth,
o palpitations of love never tamed! Accept the kiss

Qu'on sente le baiser de l'être illimité!
Et, paix, vertu, bonheur, espérance, bonté,
O fruits divins, tombez des branches éternelles!—

Ainsi vous parliez, voix, grandes voix solennelles;
Et Virgile écoutait comme j'écoute, et l'eau
Voyait passer le cygne auguste, et le bouleau
Le vent, et le rocher l'écume, et le ciel sombre
L'homme . . . —O nature! abîme! immensité de l'ombre!

*Marine-Terrace, juillet 1855.*

of being without limit! Return the kiss! And peace,
then, virtue, happiness, hope, goodness, all
divine fruits, fall from the eternal branches!

So you say, your solemn voice that Virgil heard,
as I do, and the water bore the august passage
of a swan, as did the birch the wind, the rock
the seafoam, and the universe the human mind . . .
O living world! abyss! immensity of darkness!

J'ai cueilli cette fleur pour toi sur la colline.
Dans l'âpre escarpement qui sur le flot s'incline,
Que l'aigle connaît seul et seul peut approcher,
Paisible, elle croissait aux fentes du rocher.
L'ombre baignait les flancs du morne promontoire;
Je voyais, comme on dresse au lieu d'une victoire
Un grand arc de triomphe éclatant et vermeil,
A l'endroit où s'était englouti le soleil,
La sombre nuit bâtir un porche de nuées.
Des voiles s'enfuyaient, au loin diminuées;
Quelques toits, s'éclairant au fond d'un entonnoir,
Semblaient craindre de luire et de se laisser voir.
J'ai cueilli cette fleur pour toi, ma bien-aimée.
Elle est pâle, et n'a pas de corolle embaumée,
Sa racine n'a pris sur la crête des monts
Que l'amère senteur des glauques goémons;
Moi, j'ai dit: Pauvre fleur, du haut de cette cime,
Tu devais t'en aller dans cet immense abîme
Où l'algue et le nuage et les voiles s'en vont.
Va mourir sur un cœur, abîme plus profond.
Fane-toi sur ce sein en qui palpite un monde.
Le ciel, qui te créa pour t'effeuiller dans l'onde,
Te fit pour l'océan, je te donne à l'amour.—
Le vent mêlait les flots; il ne restait du jour
Qu'une vague lueur, lentement effacée.
Oh! comme j'étais triste au fond de ma pensée
Tandis que je songeais, et que le gouffre noir
M'entrait dans l'âme avec tous les frissons du soir!

                          *Ile de Serk, août 1855.*

*Flower*

I picked this flower from the cliff for you.
On the ledge of an outcrop over the tide,
where the eagle sees himself reflected
in the calm salt pool below, it sprang
from a cranny in the rock. Shadow bathed
the flanks of the dark basalt. Overhead,
where the sun had been that day, a porch of clouds
was building up toward night. Sails dwindled
into the distance. Lamplight shone
from houses on the valley floor, as dim
as if they feared now to be seen. I picked
this flower for you, my love, though, pale,
it had no scent, or showy crown.
Its root drew nothing from the cliffside
but a bitterness like that of seaweed.
So I said, "Flower, from your deathbed here,
you would have fallen before daybreak
where the seaweed, clouds, and sails come only,
all of them, to be dispersed. Die now instead
on a human heart, abyss though it may be
yet deeper. Wither against the breast
in which a world is beating. The sky
has given you to flourish over the waves,
and by the waves be taken, but I take you
in my hand, to give you now for love."
The wind stirred over the tide,
and nothing of the day was left to fade
but afterglow. How sad it was to think,
even of you, my love, and feel that black gulf
spill into my soul with the chill of evening!

*Un peu de musique*

Ecoutez!—Comme un nid qui murmure invisible,
Un bruit confus s'approche, et des rires, des voix,
Des pas, sortent du fond vertigineux des bois.

Et voici qu'à travers la grande forêt brune
Qu'emplit la rêverie immense de la lune,
On entend frissonner et vibrer mollement,
Communiquant au bois son doux frémissement,
La guitare des monts d'Inspruck, reconnaissable
Au grelot de son manche où sonne un grain de sable;
Il s'y mêle la voix d'un homme, et ce frisson
Prend un sens et devient une vague chanson:

«Si tu veux, faisons un rêve.
Montons sur deux palefrois;
Tu m'emmènes; je t'enlève
L'oiseau chante dans les bois.

»Je suis ton maître et ta proie;
Partons, c'est la fin du jour;
Mon cheval sera la joie,
Ton cheval sera l'amour.

»Nous ferons toucher leurs têtes;
Les voyages sont aisés;
Nous donnerons à ces bêtes
Une avoine de baisers.

»Viens! nos doux chevaux mensonges
Frappent au pied tous les deux,
Le mien au fond de mes songes,
Et le tien au fond des cieux.

*Dawn at the Edge of the Woods*

Listen! Mixed with twittering from an invisible nest
nearby, confused noise drifts with laughter,
voices, footsteps, swimming out of a hidden dark,
and shadows fill with ghostlight from the moon.
That sweet shiver making the whole woods tremble
is a guitar that vibrates somewhere, as the bell
on a sleeve is plucked by a falling pebble of sand.
The voice of a man takes shape in the ear, and he sings:

> If you want, we can pretend,
> on two palfreys side by side,
> you lead me off, as I do you,
> under the blackbirds' choristry.
>
> I am your captor and your prey:
> wherever we go in the dark,
> my horse being your delight,
> yours, my pleasure.
>
> If we want them to touch heads,
> we let go the reins like this,
> and coax the animals together
> with no oats but kisses.
>
> Come! the horses stamp their hooves,
> the two of them, unreal,
> mine against the floor of dreams,
> yours on the floor of heaven.

»Un bagage est nécessaire;
Nous emporterons nos vœux,
Nos bonheurs, notre misère,
Et la fleur de tes cheveux.

»Viens, le soir brunit les chênes;
Le moineau rit; ce moqueur
Entend le doux bruit des chaînes
Que tu m'as mises au cœur.

»Ce ne sera point ma faute
Si les forêts et les monts,
En nous voyant côte à côte,
Ne murmurent pas: «Aimons!»

»Viens, sois tendre, je suis ivre.
O les verts taillis mouillés!
Ton souffle te fera suivre
Des papillons réveillés.

»L'envieux oiseau nocturne,
Triste, ouvrira son œil rond;
Les nymphes, penchant leur urne,
Dans les grottes souriront,

»Et diront: «Sommes-nous folles!
»C'est Léandre avec Héro;
»En écoutant leurs paroles
»Nous laissons tomber notre eau.»

»Allons-nous-en par l'Autriche!
Nous aurons l'aube à nos fronts;
Je serai grand, et toi riche,
Puisque nous nous aimerons.

All we need to bring along
are the true vows of desire,
and happiness, and misery,
and the loose flower of your hair.

Now, while the night swells
into the oaks, the first sparrow
jeers at the pinging of the chain
you hung about my heart.

It will not be my fault at all
if the woods and hills around us
fail to echo with my song.
Listen! Your cry answers mine!

You, be tender. Me, I'm drunk.
But o! the damp green underwoods!
where the heart's breath bears
the two of us and startled moths.

And the envious nightbirds open
their sad little eyes, while nymphs
pour sweet stuff from great urns
in sacred caves, and smile, and say:

We are possessed, like you two,
by the ancient myths of love!
and we listen to your song
and pour forth nectar none may drink.

No! I want out of the mythic woods!
The stain of dawn has spread on my brow.
And I am the Poet, and you my Muse.
What will we do here in broad daylight?

»Allons-nous-en par la terre,
Sur nos deux chevaux charmants,
Dans l'azur, dans le mystère,
Dans les éblouissements!

»Nous entrerons à l'auberge,
Et nous paîrons l'hôtelier
De ton sourire de vierge,
De mon bonjour d'écolier.

»Tu seras dame, et moi comte;
Viens, mon cœur s'épanouit;
Viens, nous conterons se conte
Aux étoiles de la nuit.»

La mélodie encor quelques instants se traîne
Sous les arbres bleuis par la lune sereine,
Puis tremble, puis expire, et la voix qui chantait
S'éteint comme un oiseau se pose; tout se tait.

We could ride into eternal blue!
Or, up the road, there is an inn,
where if you give the clerk a smile,
and I am charming, and give him cash,

while the heart's blood is in bloom,
we can shut the heavy drapes,
and count stars all day long
on the ceiling of the night.

Still the melody plays for a moment
under the trees made blue by the moon,
and after one last chord, where the voice
like a bird alights, silence clears the air for dawn.

*Orphée*

J'atteste Tanaïs, le noir fleuve aux six urnes,
Et Zeus qui fait traîner sur les grands chars nocturnes
Rhéa par des taureaux et Nyx par des chevaux,
Et les anciens géants et les hommes nouveaux,
Pluton qui nous dévore, Uranus qui nous crée,
Que j'adore une femme et qu'elle m'est sacrée.
Le monstre aux cheveux bleus, Poséidon, m'entend;
Qu'il m'exauce. Je suis l'âme humaine chantant,
Et j'aime. L'ombre immense est pleine de nuées,
La large pluie abonde aux feuilles remuées,
Borée émeut les bois, Zéphyre émeut les blés,
Ainsi nos cœurs profonds sont par l'amour troublés.
J'aimerai cette femme appelée Eurydice
Toujours, partout! Sinon que le ciel me maudisse,
Et maudisse la fleur naissante et l'épi mûr!
Ne tracez pas de mots magiques sur le mur.

*3 février 1877.*

*Orpheus*

I call as my witness the God of the blackened river
poured from six urns scorched by the fallen sun,
and the King of gods, who rides in the long car
given him by his mother's mother, Night, drawn
by oxen at noon, and later, by the horses of darkness.
I call upon you all: you giants of an earlier age;
and men of this age, which is to be the last; Earth God,
you who devour the dead; Sky God, you who breathed
breath into the forms of clay: I call you Powers
as my witness: she I worship is a woman, she
above all things is sacred. The ocean, monster
with blue hair, has granted my petition. I now
am the soul of the singing world, and I sing
love—immense, the darkness full of clouds,
the big drops bursting onto the shaken leaves,
the north wind rousing the woods, the west wind
rousing the wheat, and my mind stirred more
deeply than all these by love. For I shall love
this woman always beyond limit. If I fail:
let the sky drop curses on my head; and curse
also the flower, and the ripe ear of the wheat;
let no one ever read the magic words on the wall.

*Booz endormi*

Booz s'était couché de fatigue accablé;
Il avait tout le jour travaillé dans son aire;
Puis avait fait son lit à sa place ordinaire;
Booz dormait auprès des boisseaux pleins de blé.

Ce vieillard possédait des champs de blés et d'orge;
Il était, quoique riche, à la justice enclin;
Il n'avait pas de fange en l'eau de son moulin;
Il n'avait pas d'enfer dans le feu de sa forge.

Sa barbe était d'argent comme un ruisseau d'avril.
Sa gerbe n'était point avare ni haineuse;
Quand il voyait passer quelque pauvre glaneuse
«Laissez tomber exprès des épis,» disait-il.

Cet homme marchait pur loin des sentiers obliques,
Vêtu de probité candide et de lin blanc;
Et, toujours du côté des pauvres ruisselant,
Ses sacs de grains semblaient des fontaines publiques.

Booz était bon maître et fidèle parent;
Il était généreux, quoiqu'il fût économe;
Les femmes regardaient Booz plus qu'un jeune homme,
Car le jeune homme est beau, mais le vieillard est grand.

Le vieillard, qui revient vers la source première,
Entre aux jours éternels et sort des jours changeants;
Et l'on voit de la flamme aux yeux des jeunes gens,
Mais dans l'œil du vieillard on voit de la lumière.

\* \* \*

*Boaz Asleep*

Boaz, overcome with weariness, by torchlight
made his pallet on the threshing floor
where all day he had worked, and now he slept
among the bushels of threshed wheat.

The old man owned wheatfields and barley,
and though he was rich, he was still fair-minded.
No filth soured the sweetness of his well.
No hot iron of torture whitened in his forge.

His beard was silver as a brook in April.
He bound sheaves without the strain of hate
or envy. He saw gleaners pass, and said,
Let handfuls of the fat ears fall to them.

The man's mind, clear of untoward feeling,
clothed itself in candor. He wore clean robes.
His heaped granaries spilled over always
toward the poor, no less than public fountains.

Boaz did well by his workers and by kinsmen.
He was generous, and moderate. Women held him
worthier than younger men, for youth is handsome,
but to him in his old age came greatness.

An old man, nearing his first source, may find
the timelessness beyond times of trouble.
And though fire burned in young men's eyes,
to Ruth the eyes of Boaz shone clear light.

* * *

Donc, Booz dans la nuit dormait parmi les siens
Près des meules, qu'on eût prises pour des décombres,
Les moissonneurs couchés faisaient des groupes sombres;
Et ceci se passait dans des temps très anciens.

Les tribus d'Israël avaient pour chef un juge;
La terre, où l'homme errait sous la tente, inquiet
Des empreintes de pieds de géants qu'il voyait,
Etait mouillée encor et molle du déluge.

\* \* \*

Comme dormait Jacob, comme dormait Judith,
Booz, les yeux fermés, gisait sous la feuillée;
Or, la porte du ciel s'étant entre-bâillée
Au-dessus de sa tête, un songe en descendit.

Et ce songe était tel, que Booz vit un chêne
Qui, sorti de son ventre, allait jusqu'au ciel bleu;
Une race y montait comme une longue chaîne;
Un roi chantait en bas, en haut mourait un Dieu.

Et Booz murmurait avec la voix de l'âme:
«Comment se pourrait-il que de moi ceci vînt?
Le chiffre de mes ans a passé quatre-vingt,
Et je n'ai pas de fils, et je n'ai plus de femme.

»Voilà longtemps que celle avec qui j'ai dormi,
O Seigneur! a quitté ma couche pour la vôtre;
Et nous sommes encor tout mêlés l'un à l'autre,
Elle à demi vivante et moi mort à demi.

»Une race naîtrait de moi! Comment le croire?
Comment se pourrait-il que j'eusse des enfants?
Quand on est jeune, on a des matins triomphants;
Le jour sort de la nuit comme d'une victoire;

»Mais vieux, on tremble ainsi qu'à l'hiver le bouleau;
Je suis veuf, je suis seul, et sur moi le soir tombe,

So, Boaz slept among his heaps of grain
in darkness, as among the ruins of summer.
Reapers sprawled nearby like fallen troops.
And this took place in very ancient times.

Then, judges led the tribes of Israel.
People wandering with tents as herdsmen saw
the footprints left by giants where the earth
was soft still from the waters of the flood.

*  *  *

As Jacob slept, as Judith slept,
so now did Boaz on his threshing floor,
while overhead a door came open, and a dream
fell from the sky into the old man's mind:

he saw a live oak grow out of his belly
far up into the blue; and many people
climbed it in a long chain, while a king sat
singing at the root, and a god died at the crown.

And Boaz murmured, sleeping,
in his soul: Could this come forth
from me, past eighty? Still,
I have no son. I have no wife.

The one who shared my bed, Lord! years ago,
you took from my house into yours,
though she and I are yet one soul—hers
half-alive in me and mine half-dead in her.

And shall a nation come from this ruined flesh?
Shall I now have a child? I might believe it,
young, when I could still see mornings
rise out of the night as if in triumph.

Now, I tremble like a birch in winter.
Old, a widower, alone at nightfall,

Et je courbe, ô mon Dieu! mon âme vers la tombe,
Comme un bœuf ayant soif penche son front vers l'eau.»

Ainsi parlait Booz dans le rêve et l'extase,
Tournant vers Dieu ses yeux par le sommeil noyés;
Le cèdre ne sent pas une rose à sa base,
Et lui ne sentait pas une femme à ses pieds.

* * *

Pendant qu'il sommeillait, Ruth, une moabite,
S'était couchée aux pieds de Booz, le sein nu,
Espérant on ne sait quel rayon inconnu,
Quand viendrait du réveil la lumière subite.

Booz ne savait point qu'une femme était là,
Et Ruth ne savait point ce que Dieu voulait d'elle.
Un frais parfum sortait des touffes d'asphodèle;
Les souffles de la nuit flottaient sur Galgala.

L'ombre était nuptiale, auguste et solennelle;
Les anges y volaient sans doute obscurément,
Car on voyait passer dans la nuit, par moment,
Quelque chose de bleu qui paraissait une aile.

La respiration de Booz qui dormait
Se mêlait au bruit sourd des ruisseaux sur la mousse.
On était dans le mois où la nature est douce,
Les collines ayant des lys sur leur sommet.

Ruth songeait et Booz dormait; l'herbe était noire;
Les grelots des troupeaux palpitaient vaguement;
Une immense bonté tombait du firmament;
C'était l'heure tranquille où les lions vont boire.

Tout reposait dans Ur et dans Jérimadeth;
Les astres émaillaient le ciel profond et sombre;
Le croissant fin et clair parmi ces fleurs de l'ombre
Brillait à l'occident, et Ruth se demandait,

I have turned my soul to face the grave,
an old ox turned by thirst down to the river.

So said Boaz in his dream, his ecstasy still
turning him toward God, eyes blurred with sleep.
The cedar does not feel the rose bloom at its root,
and Boaz did not feel, at his feet, the young woman.

*   *   *

Ruth, a Moabite, had come while Boaz slept,
and now lay at his feet, who knows what light
from what door in the heavens finding her breast
naked, tender to its stirring as his dreams.

But Boaz did not know Ruth came to him,
and Ruth did not know what God asked of her.
The night breathed out a freshness from wild
clumps of asphodels over the hills of Judah.

The dark was nuptial, and august, and solemn.
Hidden angels must have hovered over them,
for Ruth saw in the night sky, here and there,
a dark blue movement like a wing.

The breath of Boaz sleeping mixed
with a dull hush of brookwater in the moss.
It was the time of year when lilies open
and let go their sweetness on the hills.

Ruth was dreaming. Boaz slept. The grass looked black.
And little bells of sheep were trembling on the verge
of silence. Goodness came down clear as starlight
into the great calm where the lions go to drink.

All slept, all, from Ur to Bethlehem.
The stars enameled the deep black of the sky.
A narrow crescent in the low dark
of the west shone, while Ruth wondered,

Immobile, ouvrant l'œil à moitié sous ses voiles,
Quel dieu, quel moissonneur de l'éternel été,
Avait, en s'en allant, négligemment jeté
Cette faucille d'or dans le champ des étoiles.

*1er mai 1859.*

lying still now, eyes half opened,
under the twinging of their lids, what god
of the eternal summer passing dropped
his golden scythe there in that field of stars.

*La Trompette du jugement*

Je vis dans la nuée un clairon monstrueux.

Et ce clairon semblait, au seuil profond des cieux,
Calme, attendre le souffle immense de l'archange.

Ce qui jamais ne meurt, ce qui jamais ne change,
L'entourait. A travers un frisson, on sentait
Que ce buccin fatal, qui rêve et qui se tait,
Quelque part, dans l'endroit où l'on crée, où l'on sème,
Avait été forgé par quelqu'un de suprême
Avec de l'équité condensée en airain.
Il était là, lugubre, effroyable, serein.
Il gisait sur la brume insondable qui tremble,
Hors du monde, au delà de tout ce qui ressemble
A la forme de quoi que ce soit.
                                        Il vivait.

Il semblait un réveil songeant près d'un chevet.

Oh! quelle nuit! là, rien n'a de contour ni d'âge;
Et le nuage est spectre, et le spectre est nuage.

* * *

Et c'était le clairon de l'abîme.
                                        Une voix
Un jour en sortira qu'on entendra sept fois.
En attendant, glacé, mais écoutant, il pense;
Couvant le châtiment, couvant la récompense;
Et toute l'épouvante éparse au ciel est sœur
De cet impénétrable et morne avertisseur.

*The Trumpet of Judgment*

I saw in the clouds a monstrous horn.

Suspended on the deep sill of the sky as if, in calm,
for an immeasurable breath. And soon: the archangel.

What never dies, what never changes,
hovered there. And here below, a thrill:
to think, this horn of doom was keeping in a dream
from outside time the hush sown somewhere deep
among the stars: justice, forged by an inhuman will
and beaten, hot, into a shape of brass. There!
There it was, in gloom, and fear, and silence.
Laid up on unfathomable mists that wobbled
out of the world, beyond all semblance
in the mind of what might be.

                                               It lived.

It dreamed the dream of an alarm clock by the bed:


all night, that night where nothing has a form or age,
and where the murk is vision, and the vision murk.

* * *

And this was the horn of the abyss.
                                     A voice
wherefrom would burst and be heard seven times,
awaiting which day, frozen, listening, the horn
broods on corrections of the soul, and on reward.
And terror, scattered in the sky, is sister prodigy
to this, which makes of indecipherable gloom a sign.

Je le considérais dans les vapeurs funèbres
Comme on verrait se taire un coq dans les ténèbres.
Pas un murmure autour du clairon souverain.
Et la terre sentait le froid de son airain,
Quoique, là, d'aucun monde on ne vît les frontières.

Et l'immobilité de tous les cimetières,
Et le sommeil de tous les tombeaux, et la paix
De tous les morts couchés dans la fosse, étaient faits
Du silence inouï qu'il avait dans la bouche;
Ce lourd silence était pour l'affreux mort farouche
L'impossibilité de faire faire un pli
Au suaire cousu sur son front par l'oubli.
Ce silence tenait en suspens l'anathème.
On comprenait que tant que ce clairon suprême
Se tairait, le sépulcre, obscur, roidi, béant,
Garderait l'attitude horrible du néant,
Que la momie aurait toujours sa bandelette,
Que l'homme irait tombant du cadavre au squelette,
Et que ce fier banquet radieux, ce festin
Que les vivants gloutons appellent le destin,
Toute la joie errante en tourbillons de fêtes,
Toutes les passions de la chair satisfaites,
Gloire, orgueil, les héros ivres, les tyrans soûls,
Continueraient d'avoir pour but et pour dessous
La pourriture, orgie offerte aux vers convives;
Mais qu'à l'heure où soudain, dans l'espace sans rives,
Cette trompette vaste et sombre sonnerait,
On verrait, comme un tas d'oiseaux d'une forêt,
Toutes les âmes, cygne, aigle, éperviers, colombes,
Frémissantes, sortir du tremblement des tombes,
Et tous les spectres faire un bruit des grandes eaux,
Et se dresser, et prendre à la hâte leurs os,
Tandis qu'au fond, au fond du gouffre, au fond du rêve,
Blanchissant l'absolu, comme un jour qui se lève,
Le front mystérieux du juge apparaîtrait!

* * *

I thought how, like a rooster in the pre-dawn dusk,
it waited, quiet in the clouds, funereal,
without a murmur, clarion-to-be of doom, and all
the earth felt cool as brass, though not one
boundary in common lay between that realm and this.

And the unstirring chill of all the graveyards,
and the stupor of the stones, and perfect calm
of corpses in the pit, was made of the unheard-of
silence in the trumpet mouth, which silence,
for the dead, was wild with the impossibility
of moving so much as their lips to crease
the sheet sown on the dead face by forgetfulness.
So, silence held the final curse in doubt.
And while the horn was keeping quiet, I could see:
the grave, as wide as it was dark, would wear
that rigid look of nothingness; the mummy
would forever have his gauze; the dead men
fall in place from corpse to skeleton.
And this proud festival of lights, this feast
which living gluttons call their destiny,
this joy that wavers in a swirl of holidays,
these passions of the flesh we consummate,
the fame, and drunken thrill of heroes, tyrants,
all would have their end and their unravelment
as meat served to an orgy of companionable worms.
But at the sudden hour when in the shoreless
gulf of space the trumpet sounds that somber
long-held note, there will be seen, as birds
that swarm out of a dark woods, all the souls,
swan, eagle, sparrow hawk, and dove, aquiver,
ushered from the trembling of their tombs,
as in a roar of swollen waters, phantoms,
rising, taking up in haste their bones.
And whitening the absolute like daybreak, then,
the apparition of the face of judgment.

\* \* \*

Ce clairon avait l'air de savoir le secret.

On sentait que le râle énorme de ce cuivre
Serait tel qu'il ferait bondir, vibrer, revivre
L'ombre, le plomb, le marbre, et qu'à ce fatal glas,
Toutes les surdités voleraient en éclats;
Que l'oubli sombre, avec sa perte de mémoire,
Se lèverait au son de la trompette noire;
Que dans cette clameur étrange, en même temps
Qu'on entendrait frémir tous les cieux palpitants,
On entendrait crier toutes les consciences;
Que le sceptique au fond de ses insouciances,
Que le voluptueux, l'athée et le douteur,
Et le maître tombé de toute sa hauteur,
Sentiraient ce fracas traverser leurs vertèbres;
Que ce déchirement céleste des ténèbres
Ferait dresser quiconque est soumis à l'arrêt;
Que qui n'entendit pas le remords, l'entendrait;
Et qu'il réveillerait, comme un choc à la porte,
L'oreille la plus dure et l'âme la plus morte,
Même ceux qui, livrés au rire, aux vains combats,
Aux vils plaisirs, n'ont point tenu compte ici-bas
Des avertissements de l'ombre et du mystère,
Même ceux que n'a point réveillés sur la terre
Le tonnerre, ce coup de cloche de la nuit!

Oh! dans l'esprit de l'homme où tout vacille et fuit,
Où le verbe n'a pas un mot qui ne bégaie,
Où l'aurore apparaît, hélas! comme une plaie,
Dans cet esprit, tremblant dès qu'il ose augurer,
Oh! comment concevoir, comment se figurer
Cette vibration communiquée aux tombes,
Cette sommation aux blêmes catacombes
Du ciel ouvrant sa porte et du gouffre ayant faim,
Le prodigieux bruit de Dieu disant: Enfin!

Oui, c'est vrai,—c'est du moins jusque-là que l'œil plonge,—
C'est l'avenir,—du moins tel qu'on le voit en songe,—

The horn had about it an air of keeping the secret.

But I could feel how one blast from that brazen throat
would shake to life the very shadow, and the plumb-bob
and the statue's limbs would vibrate till they danced,
while any deafness shivered, burst, and flew apart.
Forgetfulness itself with ruined memories would rise
into the bright black signal of that horn.
And in the eerie clamor, at the same time
as the tremblings in the rib cage of the sky,
would come the cries of every conscience: here
the skeptic in the depth of his insouciance,
and here the atheist, the doubter, the voluptuary,
here the master fallen in the fullness of his pride:
all feel doom roar into the linkage of their backbones.
And such utter rending of the shadow world
would raise whoever is within the reach of law.
The one who never heard the whisper of remorse would
hear and start up now, as when a fire-ax splits
the oak slab of a door—the dullest ear, the soul
most wholly dead, even the ones who laughed
at mayhem, groping their lovers' flesh, untouched
by any inkling of a mystery in the dark, even those
whose sleep no thunderstroke in this world ever shook!

So, if all we ever love is vanishing, or gone,
and every syllable of every word decays, and dawn
appears, unluckily, like inflammation in a wound,
how, with a mind that cowers at the thought
of prophecy, shall we conceive, much less proclaim,
the vision of what trembles up from tombs
to open in the charnel of the sky a door
through hunger into emptiness, while tumult seems
to speak the very word of God, saying: Amen!

It's true—at least as far as visions ever plunged—
Fate promises—as far as anyone can tell in dreams—

Quand le monde atteindra son but, quand les instants,
Les jours, les mois, les ans, auront rempli le temps,
Quand tombera du ciel l'heure immense et nocturne,
Cette goutte qui doit faire déborder l'urne,
Alors, dans le silence horrible, un rayon blanc,
Long, pâle, glissera, formidable et tremblant,
Sur ces haltes de nuit qu'on nomme cimetières;
Les tentes frémiront, quoiqu'elles soient des pierres,
Dans tous ces sombres camps endormis; et, sortant
Tout à coup de la brume où l'univers l'attend,
Ce clairon, au-dessus des êtres et des choses,
Au-dessus des forfaits et des apothéoses,
Des ombres et des os, des esprits et des corps,
Sonnera la diane effrayante des morts.

O lever en sursaut des larves pêle-mêle!
Oh! la Nuit réveillant la Mort, sa sœur jumelle!

Pensif, je regardais l'incorruptible airain.

\* \* \*

Les volontés sans loi, les passions sans frein,
Toutes les actions de tous les êtres, haines,
Amours, vertus, fureurs, hymnes, cris, plaisirs, peines,
Avaient laissé, dans l'ombre où rien ne remuait,
Leur pâle empreinte autour de ce bronze muet;
Une obscure Babel y tordait sa spirale.

Sa dimension vague, ineffable, spectrale,
Sortant de l'éternel, entrait dans l'absolu.
Pour pouvoir mesurer ce tube, il eût fallu
Prendre la toise au fond du rêve, et la coudée
Dans la profondeur trouble et sombre de l'idée;
Un de ses bouts touchait le bien, l'autre le mal;
Et sa longueur allait de l'homme à l'animal,
Quoiqu'on ne vît point là d'animal et point d'homme;
Couché sur terre, il eût joint Eden à Sodome.

when this world ends, when moments, days, months,
years, fill all their calendars and clocks,
and from the sky a dark beyond such measure falls,
and that last drop has overflowed the urn, then,
in the ultimate silence, one thin ray of light
will glide and tremble irresistibly across the void
into these rest stops for the night that we call graves;
then, every tent, though made of monumental stone,
will shudder in the sleep of those dark camps,
while soaring out of the mist where all creation waits,
the horn will sound above all living things
and objects, over the forfeits and redemptions,
over the shades and bones, into every mind and body,
that last harrowing reveille of the dead.

O, Sisters, hearkening out of the riot of worms!
O Night and Death, awake now, in each other's arms!

Lost in thought, I see, brass incorruptible, the horn!

\*   \*   \*

Lawless wishes, passions unreined, all pursuits
in secret of all beings, every hatred, love,
or virtue, rage or hymn, shriek, pleasure, pain,
was leaving in the dusk where nothing moved
a dim track into the horn, an inverse Babel
winding its spiral there into that silent brass.

Ineffable in its dimension, spectral, rising
out of the eternal, vaguely, into the absolute—
the measure of this horn would take a fathom
calibrated for the depths of dream, a cubit-rule
marked for the coiling gloom of abstract thought;
one end of it touched goodness, and the other evil;
so that the length went from the human to the beast,
though neither beast nor human might be seen;
yet, laid on earth, it would link Sodom to Eden.

Son embouchure, gouffre où plongeait mon regard,
Cercle de l'Inconnu ténébreux et hagard,
Pleine de cette horreur que le mystère exhale,
M'apparaissait ainsi qu'une offre colossale
D'entrer dans l'ombre où Dieu même est évanoui.
Cette gueule, avec l'air d'un redoutable ennui,
Morne, s'élargissait sur l'homme et la nature;
Et cette épouvantable et muette ouverture
Semblait le bâillement noir de l'éternité.

\* \* \*

Au fond de l'immanent et de l'illimité,
Parfois, dans les lointains sans nom de l'Invisible,
Quelque chose tremblait de vaguement terrible,
Et brillait et passait, inexprimable éclair.
Toutes les profondeurs des mondes avaient l'air
De méditer, dans l'ombre où l'ombre se répète,
L'heure où l'on entendrait de cette âpre trompette
Un appel aussi long que l'infini jaillir.
L'immuable semblait d'avance en tressaillir.

Des porches de l'abîme, antres hideux, cavernes
Que nous nommons enfers, puits, gehennams, avernes,
Bouches d'obscurité qui ne prononcent rien,
Du vide, où ne flottait nul souffle aérien,
Du silence où l'haleine osait à peine éclore,
Ceci se dégageait pour l'âme: Pas encore.

Par instants, dans ce lieu triste comme le soir,
Comme on entend le bruit de quelqu'un qui vient voir,
On entendait le pas boiteux de la justice;
Puis cela s'effaçait. Des vermines, le vice,
Le crime, s'approchaient, et, fourmillement noir,
Fuyaient. Le clairon sombre ouvrait son entonnoir.
Un groupe d'ouragans dormait dans ce cratère.
Comme cet organum des gouffres doit se taire

The embouchure, black hole where vision disappeared,
this monstrous summoning of the breath forever
into the dark where even God swoons into nothing,
wild with shadows, this colossal maw of dreariness
dilated over the world, cities and deserts,
until everything inside the opening went
mute under the black yawn of eternity.

\*  \*  \*

Out at the furthest reach of the conceivable,
and further, into the namelessness of things
unseen, a presence trembling, something vaguely
terrible, flared up, and faded, like heat lightning
on the void. And all the worldly deeps seemed
then to ponder, in that dark where darkness
sinks into itself, the hour when the trumpet
blast would break the infinite with such
a bitter cry. Immutability itself must quake.

And from the porch of the abyss, the dark lair,
from the cave called hell, from pits, Gehennas,
opened mouths of the oblivious that speak forth
nothing, from the void where no breath floats,
the mirror where no exhalation blooms, just
this released itself upon the soul: Not yet.

But, in that sad dusk, I could almost hear,
with her distinctly halting footstep, Justice
draw near for a look, and turn away. And vermin,
vice, and crime came swarming in that dark and fled.
The horn's brass whirlpool, frozen, held
a squad of hurricanes still sleeping in its cup
as in the organon of the abyss that kept them calm,

Jusqu'au jour monstrueux où nous écarterons
Les clous de notre bière au-dessus de nos fronts,
Nul bras ne le touchait dans l'invisible sphère;
Chaque race avait fait sa couche de poussière
Dans l'orbe sépulcral de son évasement;
Sur cette poudre l'œil lisait confusément
Ce mot: Riez, écrit par le doigt d'Epicure;
Et l'on voyait, au fond de la rondeur obscure,
La toile d'araignée horrible de Satan.

Des astres qui passaient murmuraient: «Souviens-t'en!
Prie!» et la nuit portait cette parole à l'ombre.

Et je ne sentais plus ni le temps ni le nombre.

*  *  *

Une sinistre main sortait de l'infini.

Vers la trompette, effroi de tout crime impuni,
Qui doit faire à la mort un jour lever la tête,
Elle pendait, énorme, ouverte, et comme prête
A saisir ce clairon qui se tait dans la nuit,
Et qu'emplit le sommeil formidable du bruit.
La main, dans la nuée et hors de l'Invisible,
S'allongeait. A quel être était-elle? Impossible
De le dire, en ce morne et brumeux firmament.
L'œil dans l'obscurité ne voyait clairement
Que les cinq doigts béants de cette main terrible;
Tant l'être, quel qu'il fût, debout dans l'ombre horrible,
—Sans doute quelque archange ou quelque séraphin
Immobile, attendant le signe de la fin,—
Plongeait profondément, sous les ténébreux voiles,
Du pied dans les enfers, du front dans les étoiles!

*15 mai 1859.*

preserved, until the monstrous day when each of us
tears through the pine lid nailed against his brow.
No hand, meanwhile, can touch in the inviolate sphere
that horn, though layered in the funerary dust inside
its bell all nations lie. I read there the commandment:
Laugh! traced by the fingertip of Epicurus. And I saw,
inside the darkest inward curve, the spiderweb of Satan.

Stars whirled by and whispered: Pray! Remember!
and the night took up their words into the dark.

And I could feel no more, either of time or number.

* * *

A dreadful hand came out of the infinite.

Toward this trumpet, which one day would make
the dead man raise his head in witness of his own
unpunished crimes, the enormous hand hung
open, yet to seize the horn which all night
filled with the imponderable sleep of sound.
Down from the Invisible the hand reached
into the clouds. Whose hand, it was impossible
to say, the heavens were so dark and hazy.
The eye in such murk made out nothing
but the gaping dreadful fingers of the hand.
This Being, whoever he was, risen in darkness—
no doubt some archangel or some seraph—
stood immovable until the Day of Judgment,
plunged under the gloomy veils,
his feet in hell, his forehead in the stars.

### Pendant une maladie

On dit que je suis fort malade,
Ami; j'ai déjà l'œil terni;
Je sens la sinistre accolade
Du squelette de l'infini.

Sitôt levé, je me recouche;
Et je suis comme si j'avais
De la terre au fond de la bouche;
Je trouve le souffle mauvais.

Comme une voile entrant au havre,
Je frissonne; mes pas sont lents,
J'ai froid; la forme du cadavre,
Morne, apparaît sous mes draps blancs.

Mes mains sont en vain réchauffées;
Ma chair comme la neige fond;
Je sens sur mon front des bouffées
De quelque chose de profond;

Est-ce le vent de l'ombre obscure?
Ce vent qui sur Jésus passa!
Est-ce le grand Rien d'Epicure,
Ou le grand Tout de Spinosa?

Les médecins s'en vont moroses;
On parle bas autour de moi,
Et tout penche, et même les choses
Ont l'attitude de l'effroi.

Perdu! voilà ce qu'on murmure.
Tout mon corps vacille, et je sens

*During Sickness*


They do not hide their hopelessness.
They say: His eyes look dull.
I feel the skeleton
that juts inside my skin.

And when I try to stand, I faint,
and lie back with a taste of dirt
that catches in my throat.
My breath disgusts me.

Like a sail that slackens at the harbor
now I shudder, seeing the form
of my cadaver shivering
under the sheet.

The nurses warm my hands, but still
my flesh feels like a snowdrift
on the bones, my forehead chilled
as if by gusts from nowhere.

This is the wind of the abyss,
cool even to the wounds of Christ!
Is it the nothingness of the Skeptics,
or is it the Great All of the Godhead?

The defeated doctors act morose,
and people at my bedside lean in
whispering, until the very objects
in the room look struck with fear.

Lost! is what they say.
All through my body I can feel

Se déclouer la sombre armure
De ma raison et de mes sens.

Je vois l'immense instant suprême
Dans les ténèbres arriver.
L'astre pâle au fond du ciel blême
Dessine son vague lever.

L'heure réelle, ou décevante,
Dresse son front mystérieux.
Ne crois pas que je m'épouvante;
J'ai toujours été curieux.

Mon âme se change en prunelle;
Ma raison sonde Dieu voilé;
Je tâte la porte éternelle,
Et j'essaie à la nuit ma clé.

C'est Dieu que le fossoyeur creuse;
Mourir, c'est l'heure de savoir;
Je dis à la mort: Vieille ouvreuse,
Je viens voir le spectacle noir.

*3 octobre 1859.*

where rivets in the armor
of my senses have burst loose.

And I can see the moment
coming for me through the shadows,
one star in a dawn-leached sky
climbing toward invisibility.

The hour of truth,
or ultimate deception, lifts
an inexpressive face, and I feel
less afraid than curious.

My soul becomes the pupil of an eye
dilating into the darkness.
Here I am. I try the door of being.
My key rattles in the night.

Gravediggers are tearing a way for me
toward God. Since death is knowledge,
to the ancient usherette I say, It's time!
Take me into the dark to see the show.

*Et nox facta est*

Le soleil était là qui mourait dans l'abîme.

L'astre, au fond du brouillard, sans air qui le ranime,
Se refroidissait, morne et lentement détruit.
On voyait sa rondeur sinistre dans la nuit;
Et l'on voyait décroître, en ce silence sombre,
Ses ulcères de feu sous une lèpre d'ombre.
Charbon d'un monde éteint! flambeau soufflé par Dieu!
Ses crevasses montraient encore un peu de feu,
Comme si par les trous du crâne on eût vu l'âme.
Au centre palpitait et rampait une flamme
Qui par instants léchait les bords extérieurs,
Et de chaque cratère il sortait des lueurs
Qui frissonnaient ainsi que de flamboyants glaives,
Et s'évanouissaient sans bruit comme des rêves.
L'astre était presque noir. L'archange était si las
Qu'il n'avait plus de voix et plus de souffle, hélas!
Et l'astre agonisait sous ses regards farouches.
Il mourait, il luttait. Avec ses sombres bouches
Dans l'obscurité froide il lançait par moments
Des flots ardents, des blocs rougis, des monts fumants,
Des rocs tout écumants de sa clarté première:
Comme si ce géant de vie et de lumière,
Englouti par la brume où tout s'évanouit,
N'eût pas voulu mourir sans insulter la nuit
Et sans cracher sa lave à la face de l'ombre.
Autour de lui le temps et l'espace et le nombre
Et la forme et le bruit expiraient, en créant
L'unité formidable et noire du néant.
Le spectre Rien levait sa tête hors du gouffre.

*Et Nox Facta Est*

There the sun was, dying in the abyss,
in a haze of shadow, no sign of resurgence,
cooled, and cooling, slowly, dismally
toward zero, disk of lesser dark
just visible in darkness, a further
diminishment in the awful silence,
ulcers of fire under its leprous
skin. Through cracks a little of the core
still showed, as if through wreckage
in a skull the human soul leaked
into view. Trembling and leaping
from within, a flame that licked out
over the surface in each crater left
small glimmerings. The star was almost
black. The archangel, so weary
that he had no voice, no breath, the star
still writhing under his last wild look,
was dying, just as the star went out.
In cold obscurity, from Satan's mouth
and from the star erupted burning floods,
scorched rubble, mountains smoldering, rocks
under the foam of primal brightness.
All around them, time and space and number,
form and sound, were dying into the lightless
unity of nonexistence. Nothing raised
its blank face out of the inconceivable.

Soudain, du cœur de l'astre, un âpre jet de soufre,
Pareil à la clameur du mourant éperdu,
Sortit, brusque, éclatant, splendide, inattendu,
Et, découpant au loin mille formes funèbres,
Enorme, illumina, jusqu'au fond des ténèbres,
Les porches monstrueux de l'infini profond.
Les angles que la nuit et l'immensité font
Apparurent. Satan, égaré, sans haleine,
La prunelle éblouie et de cet éclair pleine,
Battit de l'aile, ouvrit les mains, puis tressaillit
Et cria:—Désespoir! le voilà qui pâlit!
Et l'archange comprit, pareil au mât qui sombre,
Qu'il était le noyé du déluge de l'ombre;
Il reploya son aile aux ongles de granit,
Et se tordit les bras. Et l'astre s'éteignit.
Or, près des cieux, au bord du gouffre où rien ne change,
Une plume échappée à l'aile de l'archange
Etait restée, et, pure et blanche, frissonnait.
L'ange au front de qui l'aube éblouissante naît
La vit, la prit, et dit, l'œil sur le ciel sublime:
—Seigneur, faut-il qu'elle aille, elle aussi, dans l'abîme?—
Dieu se tourna, par l'être et la vie absorbé,
Et dit:—Ne jetez pas ce qui n'est pas tombé.—

Suddenly, from the core of the star,
a bitter jet of sulfur, like the distracted
outcry of the dying, shot forth in a splendid,
unexpected flash, cutting a thousand
funereal forms into the distance, huge,
showing on the floor of hell monstrous
porches of the infinite immensity.
Satan, bewildered, breathless, dazzled
by this lightning, flapped his wing,
opened his hands, shuddered, and cried:
Despair! It vanishes!—And the archangel
saw his own great form like a mast go down,
drowned in the deluge of God's darkness.
He folded up his wing with granite talons,
let his arms fall, and the star went out.
But, near Heaven, at the edge of the gulf,
one feather torn from the wing of the Fallen One
lay vibrant. Another angel, whose face dawn
at his birth made dazzling, saw the feather,
and stooping to take it up in hand, he said,
looking into the sublime sky: Lord, is it needful
that this too fall into the chasm? God turned,
brooding over the remnant of such glory, and said:
Do not throw down what is not yet fallen.

### La Plume de Satan

La plume, seul débris qui restât des deux ailes
De l'archange englouti dans les nuits éternelles,
Etait toujours au bord du gouffre ténébreux.
Les morts laissent ainsi quelquefois derrière eux
Quelque chose d'eux-même au seuil de la nuit triste,
Sorte de lueur vague et sombre, qui persiste.

Cette plume avait-elle une âme? Qui le sait?
Elle avait un aspect étrange; elle gisait
Et rayonnait; c'était de la clarté tombée.

Les anges la venaient voir à la dérobée.
Elle leur rappelait le grand Porte-Flambeau;
Ils l'admiraient, pensant à cet être si beau
Plus hideux maintenant que l'hydre et le crotale;
Ils songeaient à Satan dont la blancheur fatale,
D'abord ravissement, puis terreur du ciel bleu,
Fut monstrueuse au point de s'égaler à Dieu.
Cette plume faisait revivre l'envergure
De l'ange, colossale et hautaine figure;
Elle couvrait d'éclairs splendides le rocher;
Parfois les séraphins, effarés d'approcher
De ces bas-fonds où l'âme en dragon se transforme,
Reculaient, aveuglés par sa lumière énorme;
Une flamme semblait flotter dans son duvet;
On sentait, à la voir frissonner, qu'elle avait
Fait partie autrefois d'une aile révoltée;
Le jour, la nuit, la foi tendre, l'audace athée,
La curiosité des gouffres, les essors
Démesurés bravant les hasards et les sorts,
L'onde et l'air, la sagesse auguste, la démence,
Palpitaient vaguement dans cette plume immense;
Mais dans son ineffable et sourd frémissement,

*The Plume of Satan*

Of that great angel lost into the darkness
only one wingfeather was left this side
of the eternal chasm. So, the dead
may leave a vestige of themselves here
on the sill of their unending night,
a glimmer.

          Did it have a soul? Who knows?
It had a strangeness. There it lay!
It shone with remnants of the fallen light.

And angels came to see it secretly.
It brought to mind the Flaming Door.
They marveled to remember one so beautiful
made uglier by pride than any rattlesnake—
the one whose purity, at first a ravishment,
became the terror of the blue sky, monstrous
to the point of rivaling himself with God.
Such Errant Majesty! whose single feather
summoned up a vision of the whole colossus,
wingspan shading high crags from the heavens.

And at times the seraphim, amazed to draw so near
the depths where such a soul transformed himself
into a dragon, would recoil from that enormity.
A flame was floating in the feather's down,
still trembling now, as long ago,
when blasted from the wing.

Whatever tender foolishness, and god-annihilating
pride, whatever curiosity about the gulf,
or wisdom, or mere madness palpitated there,

Au souffle de l'abîme, au vent du firmament,
On sentait plus d'amour encor que de tempête.
Et sans cesse, tandis que sur l'éternel faîte
Celui qui songe à tous pensait dans sa bonté,
La plume du plus grand des anges, rejeté
Hors de la conscience et hors de l'harmonie,
Frissonnait, près du puits de la chute infinie,
Entre l'abîme plein de noirceur et les cieux.

Tout à coup un rayon de l'œil prodigieux
Qui fit le monde avec du jour, tomba sur elle.
Sous ce rayon, lueur douce et surnaturelle,
La plume tressaillit, brilla, vibra, grandit,
Prit une forme et fut vivante, et l'on eût dit
Un éblouissement qui devient une femme.
Avec le glissement mystérieux d'une âme,
Elle se souleva debout, et, se dressant,
Eclaira l'infini d'un sourire innocent.
Et les anges tremblants d'amour la regardèrent.
Les chérubins jumeaux qui l'un à l'autre adhèrent,
Les groupes constellés du matin et du soir,
Les vertus, les Esprits, se penchèrent pour voir
Cette sœur de l'enfer et du paradis naître.
Jamais le ciel sacré n'avait contemplé d'être
Plus sublime parmi les souffles et les voix.
En la voyant si fiere et si pure à la fois,
La pensée hésitait entre l'aigle et la vierge;
Sa face, défiant le gouffre qui submerge,
Mêlant l'embrasement et le rayonnement,
Flamboyait; et c'était, sous un sourcil charmant,
Le regard de la foudre avec l'œil de l'aurore.
L'archange du soleil, qu'un feu céleste dore,
Dit:—De quel nom faut-il nommer cet ange, ô Dieu?—

Alors, dans l'absolu que l'Etre a pour milieu,
Ou entendit sortir des profondeurs du Verbe
Ce mot qui, sur le front du jeune ange superbe
Encor vague et flottant dans la vaste clarté,
Fit tout à coup éclore un astre:—Liberté.—

whatever breathings-out of the abyss, or firmament,
its quivering felt more like love than death.

Unendingly, while He who minds all things thought
on His own perfections, this one feather of the angel
cast out from eternal harmony and conscience
trembled at the wellcurb of the infinite
between the dark abyss and Heaven.

All of a sudden the prodigious eyebeam
fixing the world with daylight's
preternatural effulgence fell
so that the feather shuddered, grew,
took human form, and was again
a living mystery, this time a woman.
With the look of an awakened soul,
she rose, and, standing upright, shone
into the cosmos with an innocent smile.
And trembling angels looked at her with love.
Young cherubim that hover close to one another
in the morning constellations, and at evening,
Virtues, Spirits, hung aloft to see
this sister born of hell and paradise.
The sacred sky had never yet been so sublime
as this with breathing voices. And her gaze,
an eagle's now, and now a virgin's,
shining out of the abyss that covered it,
mixing conflagration in its radiance, still
flamed. This, under a delicate eyelash,
was a look of thunder, such that Helios
himself, archangel of intensest fire,
said: Lord, by what name shall we know Her?

And from beyond the depths of human speech
in answer, out of the sources of the Absolute,
from the dim flames at her forehead floating
in the vast lucidity, one word all of a sudden
flared up into a starburst: Freedom!

*A qui la faute?*

Tu viens d'incendier la Bibliothèque?

—Oui.
J'ai mis le feu là.

—Mais c'est un crime inouï!
Crime commis par toi contre toi-même, infâme!
Mais tu viens de tuer le rayon de ton âme!
C'est ton propre flambeau que tu viens de souffler!
Ce que ta rage impie et folle ose brûler,
C'est ton bien, ton trésor, ta dot, ton héritage!
Le livre, hostile au maître, est à ton avantage.
Le livre a toujours pris fait et cause pour toi.
Une bibliothèque est un acte de foi
Des générations ténébreuses encore
Qui rendent dans la nuit témoignage à l'aurore.
Quoi! dans ce vénérable amas des vérités,
Dans ces chefs-d'œuvre pleins de foudre et de clartés,
Dans ce tombeau des temps devenu répertoire,
Dans les siècles, dans l'homme antique, dans l'histoire,
Dans le passé, leçon qu'épelle l'avenir,
Dans ce qui commença pour ne jamais finir,
Dans les poètes! quoi, dans ce gouffre des bibles,
Dans le divin monceau des Eschyles terribles,
Des Homères, des Jobs, debout sur l'horizon,
Dans Molière, Voltaire et Kant, dans la raison,
Tu jettes, misérable, une torche enflammée!
De tout l'esprit humain tu fais de la fumée!
As-tu donc oublié que ton libérateur,
C'est le livre? Le livre est là sur la hauteur;
Il luit; parce qu'il brille et qu'il les illumine,

*Whose Fault Is This?*
  (June 25, 1871)


"So: you burned the library to the ground."

"Yeah. I'm the one who set the fire."

"But, can't you see, this crime has pitted you
against yourself! These books were yours.
They fought injustice. They took up your cause.
And in return, into the depths of scripture,
onto the holy mounds of Aeschylus, Job, Homer,
into the towers of the lookouts, Molière,
Voltaire, Kant, into the very structure
of the human edifice, you throw a burning stick!
Have you forgotten that your liberator is
a book? Books are watchfires on the hillside,
beacons. In their light, the scaffolds fall.
By their say, war and hunger end.
Books say, Slavery, no more! No more
pariahs! Open a book, Plato, Milton,
read the prophets, Dante, Shakespeare, read
Corneille—the awareness living
in their language now awakens inside you.
Amazed, you find your soul in theirs.
While reading you grow sober, lucid, kind.
Their teachings enter you the way first light
breaks into an ancient cloister, and as far
as that light's burning reaches in your mind,
you feel more peaceful and alive. Their
questionings now leave you ready to reply.
You see the good inside yourself made better.
You feel old pride melting like a dust
of snowflakes by the fire, the anger gone,

Il détruit l'échafaud, la guerre, la famine;
Il parle, plus d'esclave et plus de paria.
Ouvre un livre. Platon, Milton, Beccaria.
Lis ces prophètes, Dante, ou Shakspeare, ou Corneille;
L'âme immense qu'ils ont en eux, en toi s'éveille;
Ebloui, tu te sens le même homme qu'eux tous;
Tu deviens en lisant grave, pensif et doux;
Tu sens dans ton esprit tous ces grands hommes croître,
Ils t'enseignent ainsi que l'aube éclaire un cloître;
A mesure qu'il plonge en ton cœur plus avant,
Leur chaud rayon t'apaise et te fait plus vivant;
Ton âme interrogée est prête à leur répondre;
Tu te reconnais bon, puis meilleur; tu sens fondre,
Comme la neige au feu, ton orgueil, tes fureurs,
Le mal, les préjugés, les rois, les empereurs!
Car la science en l'homme arrive la première.
Puis vient la liberté. Toute cette lumière,
C'est à toi; comprends donc, et c'est toi qui l'éteins!
Les buts rêvés par toi sont par le livre atteints.
Le livre en ta pensée entre, il défait en elle
Les liens que l'erreur à la vérité mêle,
Car toute conscience est un nœud gordien.
Il est ton médecin, ton guide, ton gardien.
Ta haine, il la guérit; te démence, il te l'ôte.
Voilà ce que tu perds, hélas, et par ta faute!
Le livre est ta richesse à toi! c'est le savoir,
Le droit, la vérité, la vertu, le devoir,
Le progrès, la raison dissipant tout délire.
Et tu détruis cela, toi!

                                    —Je ne sais pas lire.

the ill will. Emperors and kings as well
have melted. Learning comes first, later
freedom. So, all this, this light, is yours,
your strength, and you would kill it?—
though your own cause came to life in books.
Books entering into thought untied
the secret knot that error made of truth.
A book is a doctor for the mind, a guide,
a guardian. You hate, it heals. You rave
in agony, and it gives comfort. Books,
which made you rich with knowledge, freedom,
truth and virtue, duty, progress, reason
that releases the humane intelligence
from madness—all this you destroyed!"

"Yeah. What if I can't read?"

Jeanne songeait, sur l'herbe assise, grave et rose;
Je m'approchai:—Dis-moi si tu veux quelque chose,
Jeanne?—car j'obéis à ces charmants amours,
Je les guette, et je cherche à comprendre toujours
Tout ce qui peut passer par ces divines têtes.
Jeanne m'a répondu:—Je voudrais voir des bêtes.
Alors je lui montrai dans l'herbe une fourmi.
Vois! —Mais Jeanne ne fut contente qu'à demi.
—Non, les bêtes, c'est gros, me dit-elle.

                                     Leur rêve,
C'est le grand. L'océan les attire à sa grève,
Les berçant de son chant rauque, et les captivant
Par l'ombre, et par la fuite effrayante du vent;
Ils aiment l'épouvante, il leur faut le prodige.
—Je n'ai pas d'éléphant sous la main, répondis-je.
Veux-tu quelque autre chose? ô Jeanne, on te le doit!
Parle. —Alors Jeanne au ciel leva son petit doigt.
—Ça, dit-elle. —C'était l'heure où le soir commence.
Je vis à l'horizon surgir la lune immense.

From *The Art of Being a Grandfather*
   *Lesson One: The Moon*


Jeanne sat brooding in the grass,
when I came by. "Jeanne, tell me,
is there anything you want?" You see,
by looking out for them, by listening
to their wishes, I still hope
to understand the mystery
of their thoughts. Jeanne said,
"I would like to see wild animals!"
So: I showed her under the grass
an ant. "Look!" Jeanne was not impressed.
"No! Bon-papa! Wild animals are big!"

Great things occupy their dreams.
The ocean pulls them toward the shore,
rocking them in its raucous music,
hypnotizing them with shadows,
with a hideous upsurge in the wind.
What terrifies them they adore.
They feel the need to be transfixed.
"But I have no elephant on hand,
my dear. Can you think of something
else? Anything, Jeanne, tell me."
So: she pointed a finger at the sky.
"That!" she said. It was nightfall,
and I saw just clearing the horizon
the immensity of the moon.

*A Théophile Gautier*

Ami, poète, esprit, tu fuis notre nuit noire.
Tu sors de nos rumeurs pour entrer dans la gloire;
Et désormais ton nom rayonne aux purs sommets.
Moi qui t'ai connu jeune et beau, moi qui t'aimais,
Moi qui, plus d'une fois, dans nos altiers coups d'aile,
Eperdu, m'appuyais sur ton âme fidèle,
Moi, blanchi par les jours sur ma tête neigeant,
Je me souviens des temps écoulés, et songeant
A ce jeune passé qui vit nos deux aurores,
A la lutte, à l'orage, aux arènes sonores,
A l'art nouveau qui s'offre, au peuple criant: oui,
J'écoute ce grand vent sublime évanoui.

Fils de la Grèce antique et de la jeune France,
Ton fier respect des morts fut rempli d'espérance;
Jamais tu ne fermas les yeux à l'avenir.
Mage à Thèbes, druide au pied du noir Menhir,
Flamine aux bords du Tibre et brahme aux bords du Gange,
Mettant sur l'arc du Dieu la flèche de l'archange,
D'Achille et de Roland hantant les deux chevets,
Forgeur mystérieux et puissant, tu savais
Tordre tous les rayons dans une seule flamme;
Le couchant rencontrait l'aurore dans ton âme;
Hier croisait demain dans ton fécond cerveau;
Tu sacrais le vieil art aïeul de l'art nouveau;
Tu comprenais qu'il faut, lorsqu'une âme inconnue
Parle au peuple, envolée en éclairs dans la nue,
L'écouter, l'accepter, l'aimer, ouvrir les cœurs;
Calme, tu dédaignais l'effort vil des moqueurs
Ecumant sur Eschyle et bavant sur Shakspeare;
Tu savais que ce siècle a son air qu'il respire,

*To Théophile Gautier*

Gautier, your name distinct as sunlight
on the crags of mountains, I who have known you
young and handsome, I who loved you, white with days
that snow down on my head, remember now the dawn
of both of us, the contest, the arena
in a storm of voices, new art offering itself,
and people screaming. I, who hear that great wind,
the sublime, though lost, now stop you
on the funeral path to say: Go. Find truth,
you who served the beautiful. Climb
the strictest stairway. From the black bridge
over the gulf, a glimpse of arches—Go there!
Die! Soar, eagle! Leave us for a depth
more like your own—to see the absolute,
the thing itself, sublime, to feel the hurricane
roar past the summit, and from that height,
look down into the world's chimera, even Job's
great vision, even the underworld of Homer, soaring
through the mind of God to look down into Jehovah.

When one of the living leaves us, I feel how
to enter death must be to enter into the temple.
When a man has died I feel a summons
clear in his ascent for me to follow. Friend,
I see the floor of twilight crack with stars.
My thread stretched too far vibrates, touching
not quite to the sword. This wind easing you away
lifts me now to the ones who loved me in my banishment,
each fixed eye drawing me into the infinite.
Look! Here I come! Hold back the graveyard gate.

Et que, l'art ne marchant qu'en se transfigurant,
C'est embellir le beau que d'y joindre le grand.

Et l'on t'a vu pousser d'illustres cris de joie
Quand le Drame a saisi Paris comme une proie,
Quand l'antique hiver fut chassé par Floréal,
Quand l'astre inattendu du moderne idéal
Est venu tout à coup, dans le ciel qui s'embrase
Luire, et quand l'Hippogriffe a relayé Pégase!
Je te salue au seuil sévère du tombeau.
Va chercher le vrai, toi qui sus trouver le beau.
Monte l'âpre escalier. Du haut des sombres marches,
Du noir pont de l'abîme on entrevoit les arches;
Va! meurs! la dernière heure est le dernier degré.
Pars, aigle, tu vas voir des gouffres à ton gré;
Tu vas voir l'absolu, le réel, le sublime.
Tu vas sentir le vent sinistre de la cime
Et l'éblouissement du prodige éternel.
Ton olympe, tu vas le voir du haut du ciel,
Tu vas du haut du vrai voir l'humaine chimère,
Même celle de Job, même celle d'Homère,
Ame, et du haut de Dieu tu vas voir Jéhovah.
Monte, esprit! Grandis, plane, ouvre tes ailes, va!

Lorsqu'un vivant nous quitte, ému, je le contemple;
Car entrer dans la mort, c'est entrer dans le temple
Et quand un homme meurt, je vois distinctement
Dans son ascension mon propre avènement.
Ami, je sens du sort la sombre plénitude;
J'ai commencé la mort par de la solitude,
Je vois mon profond soir vaguement s'étoiler.
Voici l'heure où je vais, aussi moi, m'en aller.
Mon fil trop long frissonne et touche presque au glaive;
Le vent qui t'emporta doucement me soulève,
Et je vais suivre ceux qui m'aimaient, moi banni.
Leur œil fixe m'attire au fond de l'infini.
J'y cours. Ne fermez pas la porte funéraire.

Let me too pass; for this law none can abrogate;
all things decline; the great age like a flare
sinks in the dark where you, my friend, and I, both
vanish. What fierce noise rips out of the oaks
hewn down by Hercules at dusk for his own balefire!
As for Death, his horses whicker to themselves
for joy that such a brilliant age is ending,
such a century, that rode out every headwind,
dying . . . Gautier! you, their equal and their brother,
go to join Dumas, Lamartine, and Musset.
The legendary waters have dried up: the Styx no more
prevents us, no charmed fountain can restore us.

Lost in thought, the mower with his long blade
moves on step by step into the standing wheat.
My turn has come. My good eye, muddled now
by nightfall, straining to make out the shapes
of doves, weeps over cradles and smiles at tombs.

Passons; car c'est la loi; nul ne peut s'y soustraire;
Tout penche; et ce grand siècle avec tous ses rayons
Entre en cette ombre immense où pâles nous fuyons.
Oh! quel farouche bruit font dans le crépuscule
Les chênes qu'on abat pour le bûcher d'Hercule!
Les chevaux de la mort se mettent à hennir,
Et sont joyeux, car l'âge éclatant va finir;
Ce siècle altier qui sut dompter le vent contraire,
Expire . . .—O Gautier! toi, leur égal et leur frère,
Tu pars après Dumas, Lamartine et Musset.
L'onde antique est tarie où l'on rajeunissait;
Comme il n'est plus de Styx il n'est plus de Jouvence.
Le dur faucheur avec sa large lame avance
Pensif et pas à pas vers le reste du blé;
C'est mon tour; et la nuit emplit mon œil troublé
Qui, devinant, hélas, l'avenir des colombes,
Pleure sur des berceaux et sourit à des tombes.

*H.-H. 2 novembre 1872. Jour des Morts.*

Translator's note: Because of lines omitted near the beginning of the English version, line numbers for the French and English texts are very different. (See note on page 122.)

*Ave, dea; moriturus te salutat*

La mort et la beauté sont deux choses profondes
Qui contiennent tant d'ombre et d'azur qu'on dirait
Deux sœurs également terribles et fécondes
Ayant la même énigme et le même secret;

O femmes, voix, regards, cheveux noirs, tresses blondes,
Brillez, je meurs! ayez l'éclat, l'amour, l'attrait,
O perles que la mer mêle à ses grandes ondes,
O lumineux oiseaux de la sombre forêt!

Judith, nos deux destins sont plus près l'un de l'autre
Qu'on ne croirait, à voir mon visage et le vôtre;
Tout le divin abîme apparaît dans vos yeux,

Et moi, je sens le gouffre étoilé dans mon âme;
Nous sommes tous les deux voisins du ciel, madame,
Puisque vous êtes belle et puisque je suis vieux.

*12 juillet.*

*Sonnet*

*to Judith Gautier*

Death and Beauty, being deep, the both of them,
both jeweled with obsidian and azure, I would say
the two were sisters, fierce and rich
with the same promise, and enigma. Women,

shine to me!—voices, glances, black hair,
blond—for I am dying! I, who see your brilliance,
like the sheen of pearls that tumble in the breakers,
or like birds that flash far off in a dark woods.

Judith, our two fates have brought us closer
than we seem, to see your face and mine;
in your eyes a divine abyss appears, and I feel

in my soul a gulf plunged through with stars;
both of us belong to that same sky,
since you are beautiful and I am old.

# NOTES

*One-Year-Old:* This poem, from *Les Feuilles d'automne,* is a celebrated early expression of parental love for a small child, a more important subject in Hugo's work than in that of any major poet in France before him. My English version is a stanza shorter than the French, since I have collapsed the third-from-the-last stanza and folded it into the next-to-last stanza to avoid rhetorical flourishes that felt wooden in my voice.

*Napoleon's Army After the Fall of Moscow:* This excerpt is from one of Hugo's most famous poems, "The Expiation." This version translates most of the first of the seven sections of that poem, omitting, most conspicuously, a few lines at the beginning and a few more at the end. The translation is slightly freer than most of the others in this collection. Because of lines omitted near the beginning of the English version, line numbers for the French and English texts are very different.

*How It Happened:* For the biographical context of this poem, see the Introduction.

*All Souls' Day, 1846:* Hugo's daughter Leopoldine drowned shortly after she was married in 1843. Many of his most moving poems, including this and the next few poems here, express his grief after her death.

*The Seven Oxen of the Northern Plough:* The title of this poem in English defines the final word, which is a Greek loan word in English as in French. Hugo's title for this poem is Latin, *"Nomen, Numen, Lumen"*: name, command, light.

*Mugitusque Boum:* The title is a Latin phrase from one of Hugo's favorite poets, Virgil: "and the lowing of cattle."

*Dawn at the Edge of the Woods:* This is section eleven from *"Eviradnus,"* a narrative poem of eighteen sections. I have altered the tone and meaning of the last three stanzas in the song to make the end of the poem sufficient outside its context in the series.

*Orpheus:* English phrases that identify the gods have been substituted for the Greek names in this poem, because of the different flavor these names have now, in a world where grammar-school education in Greek and even general familiarity with the Greek gods are no longer commonplace.

*The Trumpet of Judgment:* In *The Penguin Book of French Verse, 3, The Nineteenth Century,* Anthony Hartley argues that "of all the Romantics, Hugo is without doubt the greatest." He directs the reader toward the later visionary poems as Hugo's ultimate achievement and gives this poem as an example.

*During Sickness:* Hugo nearly died of anthrax in the fall of 1859.

*Whose Fault Is This?:* For the tone of this poem the reader needs to remember Hugo's sympathy for the Commune and his position as his country's most effective advocate of social justice. Because my paraphrase of this poem felt repetitious, I have omitted about a tenth of it. Because of lines omitted near the beginning of the English version, line numbers for the French and English texts are very different.

*Et Nox Facta Est:* This version translates only the last two of the nine sections of the French poem.

*To Théophile Gautier:* Since the rhetoric of this poem, considered one of Hugo's best, lost power in my English paraphrase, this translation omits nearly half of the original. For this reason, line numbers for the French and English texts are very different.

*Sonnet:* For the biographical context of this poem, see the Introduction. The Latin title for the original poem is a variation on the gladiators' traditional salutation before combat: "Hale, goddess, he who is about to die salutes you."

# INDEX OF FRENCH TITLES AND FRENCH FIRST LINES

## FOR THE BEST IN PAPERBACKS, LOOK FOR THE

In every corner of the world, on every subject under the sun, Penguin represents quality and variety—the very best in publishing today.

For complete information about books available from Penguin—including Penguin Classics, Penguin Compass, and Puffins—and how to order them, write to us at the appropriate address below. Please note that for copyright reasons the selection of books varies from country to country.

**In the United States:** Please write to *Penguin Group (USA), P.O. Box 12289 Dept. B, Newark, New Jersey 07101-5289* or call 1-800-788-6262.

**In the United Kingdom:** Please write to *Dept. EP, Penguin Books Ltd, Bath Road, Harmondsworth, West Drayton, Middlesex UB7 0DA.*

**In Canada:** Please write to *Penguin Books Canada Ltd, 90 Eglinton Avenue East, Suite 700, Toronto, Ontario M4P 2Y3.*

**In Australia:** Please write to *Penguin Books Australia Ltd, P.O. Box 257, Ringwood, Victoria 3134.*

**In New Zealand:** Please write to *Penguin Books (NZ) Ltd, Private Bag 102902, North Shore Mail Centre, Auckland 10.*

**In India:** Please write to *Penguin Books India Pvt Ltd, 11 Panchsheel Shopping Centre, Panchsheel Park, New Delhi 110 017.*

**In the Netherlands:** Please write to *Penguin Books Netherlands bv, Postbus 3507, NL-1001 AH Amsterdam.*

**In Germany:** Please write to *Penguin Books Deutschland GmbH, Metzlerstrasse 26, 60594 Frankfurt am Main.*

**In Spain:** Please write to *Penguin Books S. A., Bravo Murillo 19, 1° B, 28015 Madrid.*

**In Italy:** Please write to *Penguin Italia s.r.l., Via Benedetto Croce 2, 20094 Corsico, Milano.*

**In France:** Please write to *Penguin France, Le Carré Wilson, 62 rue Benjamin Baillaud, 31500 Toulouse.*

**In Japan:** Please write to *Penguin Books Japan Ltd, Kaneko Building, 2-3-25 Koraku, Bunkyo-Ku, Tokyo 112.*

**In South Africa:** Please write to *Penguin Books South Africa (Pty) Ltd, Private Bag X14, Parkview, 2122 Johannesburg.*

Printed in the United States
by Baker & Taylor Publisher Services